To Liz

The broken legged Indian
Traveller !

With much love
and Commiseration.

Jenny .

A LITTLE BIT OFF THE TOP

A LITTLE BIT OFF THE TOP

A Biography of S.S. Hammersley

Barbara Jill Poloniecka

The Book Guild Ltd
Sussex, England

The Book Guild Ltd
25 High Street,
Lewes, Sussex

First published 1998
© Barbara Jill Poloniecka
Set in Times
Typesetting by
Acorn Bookwork, Salisbury, Wiltshire

Printed in Great Britain by
Bookcraft (Bath) Ltd, Avon

A catalogue record for this book is
available from the British Library

ISBN 1 85776 252 5

CONTENTS

I

A Lancashire Childhood

Werneth Hall Road, Oldham, Lancashire, forms two sides of a steep hill with The Mount, where Samuel Schofield Hammersley was born on 22 December 1892, probably on or near the crest. Unfortunately many of the house-names, which were chiselled in the stone pillars by the gates, have been erased. They are two-storeyed, semi-detached villas with steps up to a front door with a fanlight of stained glass. The main ground-floor rooms have bow windows onto a small front garden and some of the houses have long, narrow gardens at the back.

There is a photograph of Sam in a low chair, as a plump, smiling baby, with his older sister Gladys, a curly-haired, pretty child, standing smiling beside him. Their nurse Charlotte, when taking them for walks from The Mount, would probably have preferred to go in the direction of Werneth Park, away from the town. Werneth Park was then a private estate with grounds about four times as extensive as the present public park which has been made from it. The large Victorian villas in big gardens in this area still stand but then the leafy side roads ended at Hulme Grammar School, where Sam was later to go to school. Beyond the school grounds there were open fields and farms all the way to Manchester.

The other direction was, and still is, more built-up. Beyond the intersection of Coppice Street with Werneth Park Road, semi-detached villas like The Mount give way to terraces of back-to-backs in a Victorian development designed for mill operatives. The houses are close together

1

and there is a square with a church and a primary school. Yet, because the hill falls away in all directions, there is a great feeling of openness and the views over Oldham are spectacular. As Sam walked along these roads as a young boy, from every junction he would have been able to count the tall chimneys of some 50 cotton-spinning mills laid out below him.

Oldham was the centre of the cotton-spinning industry. Each mill was an imposing building of four or five storeys with a tall chimney and a tower for the vertical belts that drove the spindles. The engine house, which was often white-tiled, was usually on the side of the main building, beside the reservoir of water. From the outside they were fitting palaces for 'king cotton' but within they were both noisy and dirty. The mill floors were so slippery from the oil that lubricated the spindles that the doffing boxes, into which the spun cotton went at the end of the process, could be despatched with one kick of the clog. Both men and women operatives wore clogs and the noise they made on the cobbled roads would have been familiar to Sam since his early childhood.

These were the opulent years for cotton (between 1900 and the beginning of the First World War) in which quite ordinary men could make a fortune in ten or fifteen years and Sam's father was Chairman of seven cotton-spinning mills. In 1901, the year that Queen Victoria died and a couple of years after Sam's younger sister, Constance, was born, the family moved into the grander surroundings of Stoneleigh Hall. This was a large, square building with sash windows, on the north side of Oldham, which was built in 1869 for Daniel Grieves, a benefactor of Oldham whose monument now stands in the centre of the city. There was a formal garden, a coach house, stables and other outbuildings including a cottage, whose occupants worked in the house. Its five acres of land sloped away from the town, which was out of sight behind the hill. The moors were much closer than they were to Werneth Hall Road and the view was of open country rising

2

towards the Pennines with only an occasional farm building or mill chimney in the middle distance.

Sam was now a boy of nine. He had fair hair, light blue eyes and a fair, oval face with a short upper lip. A tinted photograph shows him in an Eton collar, knitted string tie, jacket, waistcoat and knickerbockers with knee-length socks. He was a shy child but there must have been a show-off streak in him (pushing him later to become an MP) as he would only agree to go to parties with his sisters if he could do his conjuring tricks. Constance said: 'Sam excelled with conjuring tricks and entertained all his and other friends on a Sunday evening. Sometimes I was called upon, being so unsuspecting to the audience, but I always ruined his feats as I was incapable of keeping my mouth shut.'

Sam's grandparents, the Schofields, had been musical and both the Hammersley girls inherited their talents. Gladys sang and played the piano. She was a pupil at the Manchester Music Academy and later had her soprano voice trained professionally. Constance was able to play all the latest jazz tunes by ear. Even when she was in her eighties she could hear a tune on the radio for the first time and go straight to the piano and play it. Sam's musical talent was confined to whistling. He whistled all the latest tunes harmoniously, with trills and variations.

Their father John liked company, so his friends, as well as his children's friends, would have found a convivial atmosphere at Stoneleigh Hall. He liked good food and plenty of it. Pork pie with strawberry jam was one of his favourites. He also liked sweetbreads and could eat a whole plate of them at a sitting. These were the days when people were proud to be a little stout (only the poor were thin) and the Hammersley sideboard was always loaded with food. They were also the days before central heating so feeding well helped people to keep warm.

Sam did well at Hulme Grammar School and left with a scholarship to King's College, Cambridge. Still among his books when he died was *A Treatise on Algebra* with 'SSH

Form VI' and the school motto inscribed inside, a German-language physics textbook with King's College, Cambridge, and Stoneleigh, Oldham, on the flyleaf. There was also, from his army days, a *Manual of Wireless Telegraphy* dedicated to 'Sammy with love from Gladys, Xmas 1916'.

Sam was definitely more studious than athletic and his father insisted that, as exercise, he should walk with him on the moors. It was an opportunity for them to talk as man to man, without the women of the household. A businessman and a master cotton spinner, John had many contacts and would have had an opinion on all the topics of the day. Though not an intellectual, he read thoughtfully. He was a subscriber to the Everyman's Library and made notes in the margins of the books in a small, careful hand. He was an agnostic but with old-fashioned views on such things as the place of women in society. He fiercely disagreed with his sister, who was a suffragette and a friend of Emmeline Pankhurst, who then lived in Manchester. Constance remembers the frequent and heated quarrels they had whenever she was taken to her aunt's for tea.

As father and son came home from their walks, the wind blowing in their faces, Oldham with its tall mill towers and chimneys, its collieries and ironworks and railway network would be laid out below them. The cotton trade was the next largest industry, after agriculture, in the United Kingdom. It would be taken for granted that Sam would follow in his father's footsteps and become a mill-owner too when he grew up. He and his father would have shared the prevalent belief in progress and the pride and fierce local patriotism for which Oldham was then famous. John Hammersley believed in free trade and shared the independence and the self-reliance bordering on arrogance that was characteristic of all cotton men. 'That haughty and intolerant province of Oldham', wrote Sir Charles Macara. 'They won't remove their hats except for the National Anthem'.

4

Macara's influence in Lancashire was considerable and Sam had all his books, came to know him personally and later worked with him. It was he, while he was Chairman of the Manchester Master Cotton Spinners Association, who was largely responsible for the Brooklands Agreement (Industrial Council) which successfully arbitrated between employers and operatives in the cotton industry from 1893 until the First World War. In 1924, after he retired, in an attempt to stop the run-down of the industry, he chaired the Provisional Emergency Cotton Committee on which Sam was to sit for three years before becoming an MP.

Another prominent Lancashire figure whom Sam and his father may well have talked about, was Lord Derby. Derby believed in Tory democracy and it was he who founded the Liverpool Conservative Working Men's Association at a time when many Tories were alarmed by the extended franchise, fearing that working men would not vote for them. Sam seems to have sympathised with the Conservatives because as early as 1912, when writing to his father from Germany, he added a postscript about a Conservative by-election success: 'I must not close this epistle without saying how glad I am that North-West Manchester has spoken up so well.'

He believed all his life that 'what Lancashire did today, London did tomorrow'. Even after he was married and went to live in London, and later Sussex, his loyalties remained with Lancashire and cotton. 'I doubt if any great industry had either the amount or the quality of affection spent on it by its workers that Lancashire cotton had from 1840 to 1914', wrote one commentator. 'They were cotton proud. They were cotton saturated. One generation of spinners and weavers produced the spinning and weaving masters for the next.'

This was the atmosphere in which Sam grew up. But, in spite of his commitment to Lancashire, which was reinforced by both his grandmothers and his mother being Lancastrians, the Hammersleys were not, originally, a Lancashire family. His grandfather, Henry Francis

Podmore Hammersley (who married Mary Schofield in Manchester Cathedral in 1858), was the son of a Staffordshire potter.

On the marriage certificate, Henry's profession is given as 'designer' and on his son John's birth certificate (1862) as 'china painter'. Doreen Hamer (Sam's first cousin) owns a cup and saucer hand-painted by him, but Henry aspired to being a 'real' painter (Constance had one of his landscapes). He set up in a studio but had little success and was unable to support his wife and four children. When his wife's brother, Joseph Schofield, offered them all a home, he accepted. Thus it came about that the whole family moved to Lancashire and, as Henry died of consumption while still in his forties, his children were brought up by their mother and their maternal uncle and came to think of themselves as Lancastrians.

II

Education

Today there are over ninety Hammersleys listed in the
Stoke-on-Trent telephone directory, all of them probably
relations of Homersley, who first appears in 1292, bearing
the 'Gules 3 rams heads erased or' coat of arms and
already connected with Stafford. A later Hamersley is
listed in the *Genealogical Quarterly* as having a similar
shield, and Hugh Hammersley of Staffordshire, who was
granted the crest 'a demigriffin or, holding a cross crosslet,
fitchee, gu.' in 1614, was Lord Mayor of London in 1627.
A similar crest was borne by Hugh Hammersley Esq. of
Pall Mall in 1825. Thomas Hammersley's shield (which is
among Sam's papers) also bears the three rams' heads and
the motto *Honore et Amore*.

Thomas was the son of John Hammersley and Hannah
Ball. He married Matilda Podmore and had two sons,
Richard and Henry, and two daughters, Catherine and
Isabel. It was, however, Ralph Hammersley who had the
pottery at Hanley between 1822 and 1823 and Joseph and
Robert who had it from 1877 to 1917. Another pottery
also started in 1877 called Hammersley & Co. This was at
Longton. In 1932 the name was changed to Hammersley
& Co (Longton) Ltd, and to Hammersley China Ltd in
1974. The pottery in Longton still makes 'Hammersley'
china and is now a subsidiary of Royal Worcester Spode.

Sam inherited an engraving from a portrait done by J.P.
Knight (a much sought after portrait painter) of his great-
uncle, Richard Hammersley. A letter dated 16 February
1864 to Richard from his sister Isabel, who was travelling

in Italy with her husband, Tom Seetham, congratulates him on the birth of a daughter after several sons. The Seethams had been presented to the Pope 'but there were French troops in Rome', wrote Isabel, and they feared for their safety. She mentions the 'dear boy, Joseph' and his kindness but she does not specifically say that this was Joseph Schofield, who had given her (sick) brother and his children a home.

Joseph Schofield, who was a bachelor, was, judging by his portrait, both jovial and well-fed. Like all his eight brothers and sisters who, when they were young had made up an orchestra, he was musical. The Schofields had cotton interests and at the beginning of the century they had made considerable loans to both the Soudan Mill and the Lily Mill. These loans were what we would now call shares. When Sam's father died in 1933 he still held several 'loan books' in which there were entries of interest paid, and Sam himself had 'deferred loan money' in the Broadstone Mills in Stockport which was not repaid until 1959.

When Joseph's nephews grew up he put Tom, the oldest, into banking in Manchester, where he became the first manager of the District Bank. (Later Tom married a Frenchwoman, had a son, Noel, and went to live in France.) Both Sam's father John and his younger brother Frank were put into the cotton trade. The girl, Evelyn (the suffragette), married Reginald Farnell and had two sons, Leonard and Leslie, neither of whom had any children.

Frank Hammersley's children were Hilda, Cyril and Doreen. They were close to Sam and his sisters and they saw a lot of each other. Constance particularly admired Hilda, whom she thought glamorous. Hilda became a famous golfer and her photograph is still on the wall at the Royal Birkdale Golf Club. She married Ronald Hardman and had no children. Cyril and Sam became business associates but Cyril, like his elder sister, put golf first; he never married. Doreen was 11 years younger than

Constance and as a child played both with her and with Gladys's daughter Joan, who was only seven years her junior. She married Alfred Hamer, a surgeon, and had one son, David, who likewise became a surgeon.

Sam's mother, Clara Knott, was the daughter of Robert Knott. She had one sister, whose husband Constance never felt safe with; he was, she said, 'not nice'. Robert and his wife are buried in Friezland churchyard, Saddleworth, and Sam's grandparents, Clara and John, lie beside them. In a photograph taken at the time of John and Clara's marriage, John, because he was so tall, is seated with his long legs crossed while Clara, a wasp-waisted little figure in a bustle, stands beside him; their two heads almost at the same level. In 1910 Clara died, at the age of 53. Sam was 18 at the time, Gladys was 20 and Constance was 11. It is sad to think that Clara did not live to know that her son Sam had won a scholarship to Cambridge.

Sam's scholarship was not only most gratifying to his father but also to his headmaster because in 1912, after he left school at the age of 19, Dr Hulme took him with him to Germany. The trip, however, was not considered by either of them as a holiday but a serious part of the educational process. For Sam it turned out to be a bit of an ordeal, especially early on when he was not very confident of his German. However, he did not lose his sense of humour, writing to his father that he thought he could ask the way in German in his sleep and describing the correct procedure: 'Before asking a question you give your hat a flourish and after being answered give it another flourish. He added: 'My panama is quite soiled where I get hold of it previous to giving it a short aerial voyage.' In this same letter, he wrote: 'Dr Hulme does not approve of my speaking to people who know English, hence my numerous German acquaintances.' But he broke this rule when he met two American girls on the boat going up the Rhine, who asked him to their hotel. He wrote that he was 'looking forward to a continuance of their bright and

9

extremely entertaining conversation'.

Dr Hulme made him work hard, keeping a diary of his impressions. 'There is a mild competition between us as to who can find out the most about any place', he wrote. But he had to admit that Dr Hulme, who spoke perfect German, had the edge. Their activities were not confined to sightseeing and culture. Although they did include visits to art galleries and going to concerts, they also covered visits to factories. In Heidelberg and Leipzig they went to the universities and then spent several days in the industrial city of Chemnitz (later called Karl Marx Stadt), where they tried to visit a factory. Sam wrote to his father, impressed that the various trades unions had combined to build a splendid meeting house. But he was not impressed either with the fact that, when it was opened by the King of Saxony, he told the workers that they ought to be thankful that they had such benevolent masters, nor with the true position of the unions, which, he wrote, had little freedom and less power.

He does not directly suggest that Germany was preparing for war. Yet he writes of 'the great suspicion which all our movements aroused', especially in Chemnitz with its heavy industry. They were interested in seeing over some textile works but were told there was a decree of the Chemnitz Chamber of Commerce which excluded foreigners from any factories in the town. Then the police went round to their hotel and searched their rooms in their absence. 'But luckily', wrote Sam, 'our cases were locked. The English Vice Consul was no help; he was a German, which was a farce.' They were still in Chemnitz on 2 September and witnessed the day-long celebrations for the anniversary of Sedan (Germany's victory over the French in 1870).

In October 1912 he went up to King's College, Cambridge, to read natural sciences (with German) and law. Greek and Latin were compulsory for university but Sam was not a classical scholar and said later that he only scraped by on the Greek by learning expected texts by heart. At Cambridge there was a preponderance of public school boys, especially at King's College with its many Eton endowments. But, far from being put off, Sam embraced the social advantages as enthusiastically as he lapped up the educational ones. He learned about wines, how to carve and all the latest dancing steps. He was always well-dressed and even wore white flannels and had a sweater and blazer in college colours, although he never excelled at sport.

The two pictures he had chosen to decorate his rooms (or possibly been given from Stoneleigh Hall) were neo-classical, bas-relief plaques by Harry Bates, RA. The smaller one shows Homer playing to a pair of half-clothed females and the other has a centre panel of a reclining naked Psyche flanked by two smaller panels of naked seated figures, one of whom has wings. These dreamy, romantic figures floating on clouds illustrate the idealistic side of his nature. However, he did not lack for flesh-and-blood girlfriends. He was good-looking, stylish and (an unusual advantage for those times) owned a car. But, because of college regulations at that time, his twenty first birthday dinner, which he had in his rooms, was for men only. There is a photograph of half a dozen of them standing round a white-clothed table laid out for many courses, he and his friends dressed in white tie and tails.

One of these friends was C.H.O. Williams (called Tcho). He and Sam corresponded in the holidays and throughout the war. In one of his letters, dated August 1913, Tcho wrote from Suffolk, where he had 'secured a tutorship for the Long Vac.', complaining that there was a shortage of girls. 'I thought your friend Miss Kershaw charming', he wrote, ending with: 'please remember me to your sister.'

Another Cambridge friend was Tommy Holmes, who also wrote to Sam about girls. But Tommy's was a desperate letter, from Chatham Depot Barracks, dated 22 August 1914, just before he was to embark for France. His Geraldine had not answered his letters – what had he done wrong? Could Sammy write and find out for him, he asks, but then adds: 'Perhaps you'd better not.' He was killed in action in November 1914.

Surprisingly, in spite of the interest in politics that Sam was already showing, there is no record that he joined the Debating Society when he was up at Cambridge although the President of the Union in 1912 was Philip Noel-Baker, later to become his friend. Neither did he have any contact with John Maynard Keynes, who had not yet formulated his monetary and economic theories, although he was lecturing at King's College at the time, on a stipend of £50 a year. Some years passed before their paths were to cross and Sam was to become an admirer of his, firstly in connection with his talks to the cotton trade and later in connection with Bretton Woods and the International Monetary Fund.

By the time Sam got his degree, his family had left Stoneleigh Hall, Oldham, although they had continued to live there during his first two years at Cambridge, and moved to Studholme, Clifton Drive West, St Anne's on Sea. This was not such a big house but cotton profits had slumped and John was now a widower. It was a double-fronted house on the sea-front, close to the golf club, and very soon the whole family was playing golf, together with their cousins who lived at Southport and played at Royal Birkdale.

At this time Sam's father John was the proud owner of a large open Humber which, in the fashion of the day, had a fold-down hood, huge lamps, an outside horn and wide platform steps on each side of its barrel-like body. He loved to take his daughters out for drives. But Gladys, who had the house to run, could not always come (nor did she want to) so he would take his younger daughter Constance and her little cousin Doreen. Constance remembered how they sat in the dicky wrapped up in rugs, while her father showed off how fast he could go by racing the train. For John the car was the epitome of modern living and so keen was he on this latest and exciting example of man's technological ingenuity that he even bought a garage.   The garage business was, however, short-lived.

Sam got his degree in 1915 and joined up immediately. Tcho wrote to him to HQ East Lancashire Regiment, Teignmouth, Devon, wishing that he too were in uniform. Instead, he wrote in his letter, he was still at Cambridge 'drilling three times a week with the O.T.C., coming in late and dodging the Beaks.   Heaven bless the Zeppelins; I didn't have to run.'

III

Gallipoli and the Tank Corps

Sam was tall with round shoulders; well-covered and with a full face. He had a delicate skin and a pale complexion, with fair eyebrows and lashes; large, sensitive hands with long fingers, a nose with a pronounced bridge, a high, domed forehead and rather large ears. Most of his life he wore his fair hair, which started to recede early, brushed straight back, but before 1924 he parted it in the middle. When he joined the East Lancashire Regiment in 1915, his army uniforms, with the elaborately buttoned and braided cuffs to the tunics and the cross-strap to the 'Sam Browne' belt (which was then the regulation) were of the smartest. His breeches were so pale as to be almost yellow. His shining cavalry boots, which like all his shoes were hand-made, showed off his long and narrow feet. The glass bottles in his leather dressing case had silver-plated tops with his initials, as had his hairbrushes, and he had a leather case with his initials for his silver drinking flask.

A photograph taken at Wareham Camp, where he was first stationed, shows the officers' hutted quarters with flowerbeds under curtained windows and a group in deckchairs round a large wind-up gramophone with a horn. Three of the group are Jarentzhoff, Kelly and Harold (Tich) Winder, who were later in Gallipoli with Sam. Bartlett and Clifton are in another photograph. They were killed at El Hannah in Mesopotamia in April 1916, an engagement in which Kelly and three other friends of Sam's were wounded. Also in this photograph is Lieutenant James, whom Tich reported in a letter to

Sam as having been killed on the Western Front in 1917. There are photos of Sam's platoon and of his NCOs. Sergeant Battle wrote to him later from India, where he was training conscripts (Sam had sent him a parcel), saying: 'Capt. Bull has just left for the line'. Major H.S. Bull, DSO, who had been in the 10th Battery with Sam, was killed in 1918.

In August 1915, Sam sailed for Gallipoli to join the 6th Battery and in September landed at Suvla Bay. The Dardanelle campaign, which was designed to take Constantinople and open the straights to the Black Sea, was ill-conceived by an overconfident British Navy. It did not have the support of the French and, although some seven landings were made on the Gallipoli peninsula, which is about 30 miles long, no more than a foothold was ever consolidated, in spite of most of the Turkish army being deployed in the Caucasus fighting Russia. By December it was clear that the expedition was a failure and an evacuation was ordered.

On 15 October Sam wrote to his father from 6th East Lancs, 38th Brigade, 13th Division, BMF.

My dear Pater, I hope you received my last letter to you written when we were in the support trenches. True it was more of a requisition order than a letter but perhaps for that reason I am very anxious that you should have received it. We are now in the firing line and I assure you it is far from being a picnic. We are short of officers and have all 10 hours out of 24 mapped out for duty – any spare time we use to make up arrears of sleep. Concerning our trenches, our night expeditions and military things generally, I can say nothing. Turkish prisoners are not infrequent. We never leave the firing line day or night and never take our clothes off. Still, on our immediate front one would not say that the enemy are very active though their snipers are a thorough nuisance. We have had about 15 casualties since I arrived on the peninsula, this includes one officer from my old battery, who came out the day before I did … There is one excellent thing about this battery: most of the officers are my own friends from the 10th as only two officers of the original 6th remain.

One of the chief hardships out here is the food. We get exactly the same food as the men and damn little of it. Ye Gods! I'd give £5 for a good square meal. Yet it is absolutely marvellous that they manage as well as they do. Every bit of transport has to be done at night as the line of communication to the beach from our position is under shell fire for more than $\frac{3}{4}$ of its length. If you see any nice tins of potted meat, meat lozenges or other such sustaining things, please send them along. Also please send some good throat lozenges to suck. It is frightfully cold here at night and often I am out for three hours in front of our own lines at night and it is nice to have something more to sustain one than the whizz of Turkish bullets. For this reason I want you to send out my light khaki jersey. I sent it home to you from Wareham. It is the one you got for me last winter and I thought I should not require it here. However, I find I require it very badly. In the middle of the day the sunshine brings the flies out in myriads. Today at dinner (it consisted of tea, bread and some pineapple chunks belonging to my company officer, Mr Kelly) it was absolutely, physically impossible to keep the flies off. Even if you got them all off before you got the piece of pineapple to your mouth there would be a couple sitting on it when it finally did arrive there. Some life!' Don't think, though, that it is too bad or that I am at all pessimistic. Still there is no other word for it, it's hell, perfect hell.

He then asks for 'brandy in a tin', toothpaste, and even a spirit lamp, although at the same time writing: 'I assure you it was absolutely impossible for me to bring them

16

here; as it is I have had to desert my kit-bag with all my other things on the battery dump just near the landing place.'   In conclusion, he writes:

> Give my love to the girls and assure them that I'm getting on all right.   Give my remembrance to Cook and Maggie and tell Cook that, if she wants to distinguish herself, now is the time!
> Affectionately, Sammy.

He never got the things he asked for.   The letter was not delivered until 23 November, by which time John had received a letter (dated 4 November) to say that on 20 October his son had been wounded.

Sam cabled his father himself, from the Taigne Fort Hospital in Malta.   Then there are two letters from Sammy, dated 7 and 9 November.   In the first, dated 7 November, he wrote:

> Jarentzhoff and myself had taken out a few men to try to bag a Turkish listening post which was situated 700 yards in front of our lines and 100 yards in front of the Turkish.   Practically the first few shots of the engagement winged me.   I tell you, I had a hell of a time getting back to our lines.

In the second he wrote:

> I was very glad indeed to get your wire today.   It is the first news I have received from home since I came out.   I lay on the beach on a stretcher for nearly two days before the state of the sea would allow of them getting me off to the hospital ship.   That was pretty bad.   Then on board the ship my legs seemed to get worse and worse, to swell up to a great size and get terrifically painful so that I could hardly bear to move an inch.   On the Tuesday, a week after I was wounded, they operated and ever since that time I

17

have improved ... My left leg has a wound straight through it ... The right leg has only a huge flesh wound.

While still in hospital in Malta Sam had a letter from his Cambridge friend, Tcho, who was now a schoolmaster in Edinburgh 'writing much poetry' and had decided to go into the church. Giving news of mutual friends, he wrote: 'Leslie has some photos of ourselves taken stark naked at dawn, as saints posing in one of the exterior empty niches of King's chapel.'

On his return to the UK, Sam became engaged to Trudi Ollerenshaw, whose brother had been at Cambridge with him. Jarentzhoff wrote to Sam on 15 April, 1916: 'congratulations on your engagement' and Tcho finished one of his 'until I see you again at your wedding with Miss Ollerenshaw. Wait until I'm priested and I'll be honoured to do the deed for nothing.' But Tcho was never called upon, as the engagement was broken off and the gold ring Sam had bought for Trudi he eventually gave to Eleanor Maunsell.

Eleanor was the schoolgirl granddaughter of Mrs Nantes of Bridport, where Sam was billeted when he returned to his regiment after convalescing with his family at Studholme. He became very fond of her, took her out from her boarding school at Weymouth and bought her presents. When he met his wife-to-be, he told her: 'Eleanor is a darling child, you will love her', and when eventually Eleanor married, she married a man who looked not unlike Sam. She was godmother to Sam's eldest child and Tcho was the godfather.

Sam's wounds healed completely, leaving him without any trace of a limp (although throughout his life, particularly in wet weather, he was to get painful rheumatic twinges in his left leg). When not on duty, he started going regularly to tea dances at the Linden Hall Hydro in Bournemouth, run by Leo and Queenie Exton, who became his friends. Two of the emancipated young

18

women he danced with there were the McCarthy girls, one of whom married Ronald Bodley Scott, later to become the Queen's physician. They introduced him to Basil Groves and William Jefferson Wakley, called Jeff, who was a friend of Walter Wilson, the inventor of the tank.

Jeff and Basil were stationed, as Sam was, at Bovington Camp, near Wareham. Both were engineers and already in the Heavy Branch Machine-gun Corps. This was the unit working with the then secret and experimental new weapon, a 'cross-country armoured car of high offensive power' that in February 1915 the Landships Committee had been set up under the Admiralty to work on. Between March and September 1915 teams of mechanical engineers, both military and civil, worked on a variety of experimental vehicles to produce something with firepower, armour and manoeuvrability. When Walter Wilson combined his epicyclic gearbox with William Tritton's track-laying mechanism, the tank was born and Albert Stern, with whom Sam was to work on tank development in the Second World War, virtually forced the British Army to adopt it.

The first tank was a cumbersome, noisy thing with poor visibility. The driver only saw straight ahead. When he wanted to move to the left or right he held out his hand to the left or right and the appropriate track-man changed the direction of the tracks. Another man, sitting beside him, moved the tank up or down. The huge engine was in the middle and was very hot and so noisy that the crew could not talk to each other. There were two gun-turrets, mounted on the sides, each requiring a separate operator.

Secrecy surrounded the development of tanks and the first ones to go into action, in September 1916, were still with the Heavy Branch Machine-gun Corps. It was only when an abandoned tank called HMS *Corunna* was reported in the French press that their existence was acknowledged publicly. Sam had transferred from the East Lancashire Regiment to the Tank Corps as soon as recruitment started. However, tanks were not at first a success, either mechanically or tactically. They were used in unsuitable terrain and broke down. During the greater part of 1917, he was salvaging tanks which, in his own words 'were lost, out of action, or submerged in that quagmire of earth known as the salient of Ypres'. They were useless in the Flanders mud when they were committed at the Battle of the Somme in September 1917.

It was not until 20 November of that year, at Cambrai, that the tanks really showed what they could do. Then the ground was hard and dry and they went into battle without a preliminary bombardment so as to maximise the element of surprise. They advanced five miles, crossed all three German lines and made a gap in the German defences four miles wide. Some 10,000 German prisoners and 200 guns were taken and, although British losses were 1,500, such was the success that church bells were rung in London for a victory.

Jeff Wakley, however, was not rejoicing; he was by then in hospital, having been wounded when the British retook Bapaume on 17 September. He lay three days in a foxhole before being rescued, by which time his leg had become gangrenous and had to be amputated. He refused to wear the wooden leg he was offered and to the end of his life hopped with the aid of two crutches. He was not, however, discharged from the army but was sent to the War Office to the Mechanical Warfare Department, where he worked with Colonel Knothe on tank development.

IV

Romance

In November 1917 Sam got leave and went up to London
to visit Jeff in his Bayswater flat and Jeff introduced him to
his sister Kit, who was keeping house for him. Kit and
Sam fell in love. They only danced once before he
proposed. He sent her flowers, and chocolates from
Charbonnel & Walker. When he could not get away to
London to take her dancing at the Savoy or the Berkeley
Hotel, he sent her telegrams, sometimes two or three times
a day. He wrote her long, romantic letters, signing himself
'your devoted knight' and calling her 'the most beautiful
woman in the world'.

Five years younger than Sam, Kit had a narrow face with
a straight nose, a firm chin-line and hooded eyes. She was
small-boned, with shapely legs and ankles, very slim, and,
although she had square shoulders she rebelled against
Edwardian deportment, stooping, so that one of the first
times that they went dancing Sam, who also stooped, told
her: 'all our children will have round shoulders too!' She
also, in accordance with the fashions of the 1920s, looked
flat-chested in the early married photographs, which show
her in loose dresses with drop waists.

The first letter that she wrote to Sam was from her
stone-deaf, Burbrook grandmother's. She was, she wrote,
obliged to play halma with the old lady (Sarah Adelaide,
née Hilton): 'but Granny cheats and then, when she's won,
tells me where I've gone wrong!' The granny's house and
that of the aunts were just across the fields from one
another, in Hatfield Heath. Kit had lived with her

Burbrook aunts, on and off, ever since her mother died, when she was 11. They were her mother Helen's four sisters (one of whom, Margaret, had married Sir Sigmund Dannreuther). On this side of her family Kit was a descendant of Richard Vere Hunt, vicar of Medmenham, whose daughter Emma had an illegitimate son. The Burbrooks were very poor and very proud. The eldest of them, after Kit's mother, was Mary (called Ja), who had fallen in love with an Indian when she was young but did not think it right to marry him.

On her father's side, Kit was descended from Charles Wakley, brother of Thomas Wakley, JP, MP, who founded *The Lancet*, in 1823, 'to attack medical abuses'. Her Wakley grandmother, Eleanor Sarnia Jones, came from a well-off Guernsey family. She was a good businesswoman and acquired property in the Birmingham area as well as in Guernsey, which she entailed. Neither Kit's father, William Robert, who had been in the navy and retired to Guernsey, nor either of his two brothers, nor his sister, could get at the capital. One brother, Bernard (who died in 1925), was married but had no children. Tom and Nell, who were younger, never married. They all lived frugally (together with their mother until her death in 1901) in a large house in Kensington. During the Great War, Nell, who was known in the family as a miser, wore a belt hung with gold sovereigns, and after her death in 1942, more sovereigns were found stuffed into the cushions in her sitting room. Tom did not die until 1951. He was a solicitor and 'managed' the Wakley properties in Birmingham but, although he collected the rents, he spent no money on their maintenance.

Kit's life in Guernsey as a girl had not been easy. Her father drank and was short-tempered, going off on drinking bouts with his friend Jefferson (after whom he named his son). Her mother was gentle, like all the Burbrooks, and played the piano. Most of William Robert's aggression was directed against his son Jeff, who was sent as a boarder to St Paul's School, Hammersmith, which he hated. After his mother's death Kit's maternal aunts gave her a home but she did not feel safe there because her father, when sober, would suddenly remember that he had a daughter and demand that she be sent to him. She, therefore, see-sawed between the genteel poverty of her aunts' house in Hertfordshire and the complete freedom of her time in Guernsey with him. Guernsey was not, however, only freedom, it was neglect because, after making a big fuss of her for a day or two, her father forgot her again and, but for the kindness of the neighbouring farmers, the Chilcotts, whose beets she chewed raw, Kit would not have had enough to eat. Once, when the Chilcotts had taken her to church with them, her father stormed in and removed her in the middle of the service. Even at her convent boarding school, near the aunts, where she was happy and had a crush on a Sister Teresa, she did not feel secure, knowing that, even in term-time, he might suddenly demand that she go back to him in Guernsey.

Jeff joined his father and Kit at La Quevillette farm in Guernsey for his holidays but when their father died, in 1922, he sold it to the Chilcotts. Kit adored him but he teased her, forcing her to do dangerous things that frightened her, like walking a cliff path that crumbled, making her leap across chasms and climb heights. She had mixed feelings about Guernsey and although she talked about it as a place she loved, yet she never took her children there on holiday and all her life rebelled against having to make the Channel crossing. She was, however, fiercely loyal to Jeff, although neither of them was entirely honest with the other. It was only when the business of the Wakley estates came up in the late 1950s that her faith in him was shaken and she allowed herself to see him in another light.

When the First World War broke out she had left school and was already rebelling against boredom and the restrictions of life with her Burbrook aunts, who didn't know quite what to do with her. She discarded her long skirt, had her hair bobbed and, after a brief period at a

23

gymnastic academy, where she met Madge Everitt, who was also training to be a PT instructor, she got a job as a clerk. Male clerks were rapidly being replaced by females, largely due to the wartime need to release men to work in munitions, but partly thanks to the militant suffragettes who had been demonstrating for women's 'right to work' ever since 1913. Kit got a job in the Ministry of Agriculture for the Potato Board and went to live with Jeff in London.

However, although she kept house for her wounded brother, she was not always wanted at the Bayswater flat. 'Jeff doesn't want me when Eve can come', she wrote to Sam, 'but demands me and curses me when she isn't there.' Eve La Touche, who was a VAD, was in love with Jeff, although there is a letter from him to Kit in which he writes that they are 'just good pals'. Eve was married, with a schoolboy son. When her husband was at the front, she came and lived in Jeff's flat. Kit must have heard that La Touche had killed a man because she wrote to Sam saying: 'I hope he doesn't come and kill Jeff!'

Although he had introduced her to Sam, Jeff discouraged Kit from going out with him, telling her that he was a philanderer. The Wakley family did not think him good enough for her. In one of her letters to Sam, Kit wrote: 'Aunt Nell has just suggested that you are going to run away with another girl, she says there must be plenty in Bournemouth.' And in another: 'Jeff is beastly about you.' Jeff made snide remarks, asking her: 'are you expecting the fish train from the North?'

Something of what they felt about him must have got through to Sam because after they were engaged he wrote to Kit: 'it is wonderful that you should love a big, selfish, plebeian, conceited, mountebank like me.' From the time of their first meeting, they wrote to each other almost every day. Soon Sam had a photograph of her in his cubicle, which he kissed before going to sleep at night. He stayed in camp rather than go to the Linden Hall Hydro as he used to, because, he wrote, he did not want to dance

24

with anyone but her. He appointed her an imaginary bodyguard, called Ichthyboskoi, who was to watch over her. Then various other funny beasts were suggested, including the Poffel. In one of his letters he wrote out a verse about the Poffel, which he took from a book he had bought as a present for Eleanor Maunsell. But as the conclusion was that the animal had no son or daughter, 'it is not for us', wrote Sam.

Many of Sam's letters were very romantic and in at least one of hers Kit writes back that she is scared that she cannot live up to his idea of her. But they also teased each other. Kit wrote to him about his double chins and he wrote back to say that previously there had been four of these but there were now seventeen! She also teased him about his 'abominable abdomen' and he accused her of being duck-built because she wanted to wear very high-heeled shoes. She obviously needed to talk about him to somebody and wrote that she had asked her granny if she liked fat men with double chins and white eyebrows, shouting this down the old lady's ear-trumpet. Sometimes she wrote to him as 'my knight' but more often it was 'prawn'. (They had been together in Dorset during the summer and his fair skin reddened in the sun but never browned.) 'I should love to be silly with you, my funny, pink prawn', she wrote. 'You are such a topping fool and it's so comfy to be a fool with a fool. I wish you were here.' In the short period between 20 November 1918 and 21 January 1919 he sent her thirty letters and nine telegrams, one of the telegrams simply to ask: 'Have you given the Ichthyboskoi his food?'

In October 1918 Kit, Eve and Jeff were all ill with Spanish flu at Jeff's flat. Sam too got it while on leave in London. When he recovered he went up to St Anne's on Sea, to his father and sisters. He told Gladys that he was planning to marry Kit, writing: 'I have talked to her about you and shown her your photo. I know I said I wouldn't but she is the person to whom I tell most things.' Gladys had recently been married herself and her husband, Percy

Birch, had gone back to France, leaving her pregnant. He was killed in the last days of the war and never saw his daughter, who was christened Joan but later called Joanna.

Sam must also have told his father that he planned to get married and been advised to get settled in business first, because in another letter from this same Leave, he wrote to Kit: 'I have only just finished a frightful argument with my father who has dubbed me a pacifist and lacking in the most elementary principles of business acumen.' John, like Sam himself, was not easily angered but when he was, he became red in the face and very angry indeed.

V

Marriage

By the time the First World War came to an end on 11
November 1918, Kit and Sam were already making plans
for their wedding. Kit's job in the Ministry of Agriculture
came to an end and she returned to Hatfield Heath, taking
Sam down to meet her grandmother and aunts. Sam was
not yet demobbed so, like all service personnel, had to get
written permission from his commanding officer before he
could marry. But this was not a problem. Lieutenant
Colonel H.W.B. Thorpe (whom Sam called 'Daddy Thorpe'
although he was a bachelor) knew and liked Kit. Sam
wrote to her to say that they had stayed up until 2 a.m.
'talking about you'.

Just before Christmas, he collected Eleanor from school
and brought her up to London to take her, with Kit, to
see *Peter Pan*. Kit was not pleased, eliciting a letter from
him that explained: 'Eleanor is just a child. My love for
you is the only great thing in my life.' In another letter he
wrote: 'when anything happens which seems to put off, or
threaten, or delay our marriage, I get miserable.'

At Christmas he sent her two engagement rings to
choose from and she sent him a silver cigarette-holder.
However, they did not spend the holiday together as he
had to stay in camp as duty officer, responsible for
organising entertainments, meals for officers, NCOs and
men and a football match. Before serving the men's
Christmas Day dinner, he made a speech. He also had to
take church parade. 'When I am in church I shall think of
you,' he wrote to Kit, 'and pray (I don't know to whom)

27

that I may be worthy of you and make you happy.'

At New Year Kit and Jeff had an invitation to stay a few days with the Walter Wilsons, where there was to be a dance. Walter and his wife Ethel were very kind and supportive to Kit and Sam, as well as to Jeff, and they and their three sons were their lifelong friends.

At Tank Corps Headquarters demobilisation had already begun. Sam wrote to Kit that his friends Dunlop and Medlicott had been demobbed and had come to say goodbye. He had a letter from S.L. Williams, who had also been demobbed, to say that he was going to Canada 'as there seems little chance to get a decent job in Britain'. A few months later Williams wrote again, very pleased with life, from Winnipeg, where he was working for the Canadian Northern Railway. In British Columbia he had received a hero's welcome but he had not stayed there because he found it too quiet.

Sam wrote to Kit on 14 January that there was unrest at Bovington: 'Daddy Thorpe is depressed. He has trouble with the men. There are refusals to work and refusals to parade. There is really no work to do. Just a matter of sheer wind-up. I have been tramping through the mud to see to the arrangements for the arrival of the tanks we have to store. But', he went on in a more cheerful vein, 'I am due a month's Leave, which I suggest we should spend down here looking for a house.' Writing from Central Workshops, but on Savoy Hotel notepaper, he says: 'the McCarthys will invite you and we can stay in Bournemouth. What do you say, you darling devil?'

Kit thought it would be nice to live at Lulworth Cove and, knowing that his father wanted him to get settled in business before he married, she encouraged him to look for a business in Bournemouth. Sam answered the letter in which his father said, 'if you get demobbed I will find you a business and you can get married' by writing: 'if you can find a business immediately – good! If not, I propose to get married and find a business afterwards.' Then, shortly after this exchange of letters, his father found a business

28

for him in Blackpool. But he did not get it as there were two other people bidding for it at the same time. Then Sam wired to Kit that the Bournemouth visit to the McCarthys would have to be postponed because another business had come up, this time in Oldham, and it looked very promising. Would she come with him to St Anne's?

Kit agreed. When earlier she had been apprehensive about going to live in the north, her widowed Aunt Kathleen (née Burbrook), who was more sympathetic and encouraging about her marrying Sam than the Wakleys were, wrote: 'there is a very intellectual and refined circle in Lancashire that counteracts the vulgarity of the nouveaux-riches, also the musical circle.'

Gladys would have agreed with this. She belonged to the musical circle, with friends from the Manchester Music Academy, where she had trained as a singer. After being persuaded to go to Blackpool for the Victory Ball, she wrote to Sam to say that it was an experiment she would not want to repeat 'with all those flashy, vulgar women'. Since the death of their mother she had been keeping house for her father and her younger sister and, now a young widow, was awaiting the arrival of her baby.

But, although Kit's aunt Kathleen had written: 'you will like them [the Lancastrians] they are so good-hearted', at first Kit was ill at ease with her future in-laws, in spite of the warmth of their welcome. Her lifelong feeling of insecurity made her suspicious. She was also very competitive and felt at a disadvantage with her shortage of formal education, and, although she was sufficiently quick-witted to make up for this in general conversation, she was always expecting to be found out. Elsie Corlett, who, like Sam's cousin Hilda, played golf for Lancashire, was a regular visitor for Sunday lunch at Studholme. Everyone except Kit played golf, even Constance, who, indulged by her father, at 19 had her own car and did exactly as she pleased.

Kit, however, was prepared to live in Lancashire as long as she could get married; where they lived or what he did for a living, she told Sam, were of secondary importance. But back at Bovington Camp, Sam got another telegram from his father: 'Want Cyril to be partner. Wire if don't agree.'

Sam did not agree and wired back: 'Willing to go in myself. Unwilling to have partner.' However he was overruled and had to accept his cousin, since Cyril's father Frank also had profits to invest and wanting to get his own son started in business.

They were all agreed that the Oldham business had good prospects. It was called S. Noton & Sons and was a going concern making fibre and metal canisters for the cotton industry. No connection, however, is known between the name of this business and William Noton, who was a co-director with John Hammersley at the Delta Mill and the Lily and whose family were shareholders in a number of the Hammersley cotton mills.

On 10 March 1919, Sam and Kit were married. The wedding was in London, at the Chapel Royal of the Savoy. He was still in uniform. Their first house, near Altrincham, was called Beech Hurst. Kit stayed at Studholme while Sam got it ready for her. She wrote to him in June: 'I sought cooks all morning. Has all the furniture come? I wish I had come with you.' The letter was addressed to 'Bundy-Boo' and signed 'Wiffalums'. She had, she told him, bought a mat of cut-up motor tyres for outside the front door, made by disabled soldiers. The next day she wrote again: 'Have engaged Florence – a treasure. Maggie's girl says she'll come as housemaid.' She also asks after Tartar, the dog, whom Sam had taken with him. Sam answered her with a letter from the Midland Hotel in Manchester and a telegram with the single word 'tremendously' from Oldham, both signed 'Bundy-Boo'.

In May 1919 Sam was notified that he had been released from active service and put on the Reserve. By January 1920 they were settled into the house, Beech Hurst notepaper was printed and Sam wrote a poem on it entitled 'Winter Firs'. He then turned his attention to his Norton's business, giving his old Tank Corp Sergeant, Henry Orford, a job there, and in May visited Rotterdam, The Hague and then Hamburg to investigate the latest vulcanised-fibre processes. By the end of the year he was writing from Belfast, where he had gone to find new markets for his canisters: 'ever since we landed this morning I have been going round to dusty flour mills interviewing dustier flour-mill managers and talking – talking – TALKING. I send both of you my dearest love.'

'Both' because on 5 December their first child, Penelope Anne, was born. Sam arranged for Kit to go to an expensive nursing home in Woking to have the baby. But she did not like the restrictions so, after the birth, she persuaded him to take her away, so that they could be together. He was only too ready to indulge her and, as being looked after and made a fuss of was exactly what her life had lacked so far, she let him install her in a suite at the Berkeley Hotel, Piccadilly, with the baby and a nurse. When Penelope cried, Sam danced with her in his arms. (Kit had trouble breast-feeding her at first.)' He loved babies and had a calming effect on them, dancing in turn with each one of them when they were tiny. Then Kit went down to Bridport, where her friend Madge Everitt stayed with her at Cliff Cottage, West Bay. Beech Hurst was closed and Sam wrote to her from the Midland Hotel in Manchester, indulging his love of playing with words, complaining of the other hotel inmates: 'a more cock-eyed collection of brass-bummed bandits was never housed in any hostel'.

Sam had a bookplate designed for him which depicted a draped statue of a woman without arms, like the *Venus de Milo*, superimposed on rows of books, a tank surmounted by a sword, a bag of golf clubs, a hammer and a tall fibre canister of the type S. Noton and Sons made for the cotton trade. A baby's shoe was in the bottom right-hand corner.

In January 1922, he went with his Schofield cousin to

cotton mills near Lille. From there, before going again to Hamburg, he wrote to Kit: 'this is a place about four times worse than Oldham, snow on the ground, water in the air and people chattering all around like monkeys.'

On 5 March his second daughter, Barbara Jill, was born. (Penelope Anne was only six months old when Kit had found that she was pregnant again.) But they all went to Stroud to stay with Jeff, who was now married to Eve, where the new baby, who was about six weeks old, caught pneumonia. The doctor prescribed brandy, to be given to her from a pipette, and said that Kit should stay on hand to breast-feed her on demand. Kit needed a responsible nanny for 'Baby' and 'Tiny Baby', and Edith Poulton was engaged. Edith (Nanny) was a farmer's daughter from Wiltshire, one of ten children. She took full charge from then on and stayed with the family until after all the children had grown up.

In July 1923 Sam had to go and do his military training, for which he was attached to the 4th Tank Battalion. On his return he wrote, as requested, to give the War Office his impressions. 'From the point of view of a fighting officer,' he wrote, 'I would say that at the present time officers will obtain the greatest advantage by concentrating on gunnery during the period of their attachment.' His reasons were: '(1) tank training to an officer of the Reserve is not at present much value in view of the obsolescent character of the existing tank and (2) gunnery is the basis of the fighting efficiency of the tank.'

In September he moved his family to a larger house, The Beeches, also in Altrincham, and Mina McKenzie came as parlourmaid. To the other staff she was Miss McKenzie but to the children 'Kenzie'. She also stayed with the family, on and off, until she retired. Like Sam, she loved music hall songs and they used to sing Murray and Leigh's *A Little Bit off the Top* together as she brought the Sunday joint into the dining room for Sam to carve. She also sang the Lancashire songs with him, like *The Return* (of Fred Fannackerpan) and *Sam, Sam, Pick up tha Musket*

with its invitation to the King: 'when tha's next in Lancashire tha's having tea with me', as well as Gracie Fields
songs such as *Granny's Little Old Skin Rug* and *The
Biggest Aspidistra in the World.* Nanny occasionally sang
Marie Lloyd's *Oh, Mr Porter* but mostly she sang hymns.
There is a photograph of Nanny and Kenzie, each in long,
dark skirts and white blouses with mutton-chop sleeves,
standing in the garden at The Beeches with the two little
girls in front of them and the third daughter, Priscilla Jane,
who was born in 1925, in Nanny's arms.

VI

Member of Parliament for Stockport

By 1922, when Sam's father gave him a seat on the board of two of his cotton mills, cotton prices had slumped. But John, in common with many others of his generation, believed that the short-time working and massive unemployment, like the disabled soldiers who were begging on the streets, were just an aftermath of war and that the Lancashire cotton trade would recover. However, the government's policy of deflation and free imports hit Lancashire particularly badly and Sam believed that as long as bankers and politicians talked of returning to the gold standard and reducing the money supply, the situation would not improve.

From October 1922 through 1923 he had letters published in the *Manchester Guardian*, the *Manchester Evening Chronicle* and the *Daily Chronicle*, with financial suggestions both for improving the economy and restructuring the cotton-spinning industry. He also spoke at the annual meeting of the Cotton Federation, got a seat on the committee of the Oldham Master Cotton Spinners Association and became a member of the Provisional Emergency Cotton Committee under the chairmanship of Sir Charles Macara.

The objective of this last committee was to get a single body to control the industry so that its members would not undersell each other. The new scheme had to be compulsory because, under the Federation's voluntary arrangements many mill-owners ran longer working hours than had been agreed and did not co-operate, fearing that they

34

might be disadvantaged if they submitted statistics when some mills did not. They failed to see the strength of foreign competition and continued to reduce their profit margins, both in weaving and in spinning, undercutting one another.

Sam sat on the Provisional Emergency Cotton Committee for three years, trying to get agreement throughout the industry. But it was not only mill-owners who were individualists, the operatives were too. They were against short-time working and afraid of loss of earnings. Besides, there was rivalry between Sam's committee and the more powerful Federation of Master Cotton Spinners Association, which was recognised by the government, and of which Macara had previously been chairman.

In an attempt to break the deadlock, Sam proposed that Macara should become titular head of both committees. But Lady Macara was afraid that this would be too much for him to take on because of his age, and spoke to Kit about it. Macara wrote to Sam at The Beeches, saying that, although medical advice was against it, he was ready to do anything to save the industry for which he had worked so hard for 40 years.

However, without backing from the banks, which, like government, would only talk to the Federation, the Provisional Committee's scheme was doomed. There were even cries in some circles of 'illegal restraint of trade' and, because government had intervened in the country's economic life to an unprecedented degree during the war, many thought that the best reaction was to get rid of all interference and leave everything to free trade.

A further disadvantage with which the cotton trade was saddled was that when big profits were made during and immediately after the war, many mills had increased their loan capital, believing that good times were back to stay. The boom, however was short-lived and by 1921, when demand in Europe fell off, most cotton mills were in debt to the banks. These were reluctant to cut their losses and kept a stranglehold on the industry. Also the cotton trade, like other basic industries, was slow to adapt to a changing world.

The following appeared in both the *Oldham Chronicle* and the *Stockport Advertiser* under a picture of Sam in a butterfly collar, striped trousers and spats.

> Like his father, Mr Hammersley takes more than a passing interest in the cotton spinning trade. He is on the boards of the Fern and Rex Spinning Companies. He is generally regarded as one of the men – too few in number for so great an industry, we are sorry to say – who are able to take a wide view of the problems that lie in front of Lancashire's greatest trade. There are many men who can successfully run their own businesses but their training has not been such as befits those who should be statesmanlike leaders of a great department of the nation's work and life.

Sam attracted the attention of Lord Derby and, with his support, was adopted by the Conservatives to contest the two-member seat of Stockport at the December 1923 parliamentary election. He did not, however, get in. The first-ever Labour government was elected but, as Ramsay MacDonald's administration was heavily dependent on Liberal support, it was short-lived. (During the 1920s and 1930s the proportion of Liberal seats in parliament was about one-third of the whole.) When another general election was called in October 1924, Sam stood again and, on an 86 per cent poll, got in, together with his fellow Conservative William Greenwood. Jointly they thanked their supporters in an illustrated handout, which said:

> You realised that the foundations of the nation's prosperity were threatened by the proposed legislation of the Socialists and, mindful of the danger in which the Country stood, you exerted yourself to secure a practi-

cal and stable Government. Success crowned your efforts and for the first time in twenty nine years Stockport is represented in the House of Commons by two Conservatives.

Sam was 33 years of age. He made his maiden speech on 26 March 1925, on one of the great issues of the day, unemployment, particularly as it affected the cotton trade. At this time Stockport, on the river Mersey, was a county borough with a population of about 124,000, of which some 38,000 were unemployed. Cotton was the chief industry. The Prime Minister, Stanley Baldwin, opening the debate, had spoken on the need for government/industry discussions. This Sam heartily endorsed, saying that ever since 1921 there had been massive unemployment in the cotton trade and the industry was now running at only 75 per cent of its pre-war capacity.

While acknowledging that the cotton industry needed to reorganise, he took up a point made by Robert Boothby, who had also made his maiden speech earlier in the same debate, namely the need for stable prices for raw materials. He was himself, Sam said, carrying out experiments in the use of short-staple cotton from India in an attempt to replace the shortfall of expensive American long-staple cotton. Lancashire still had one-third of the total spindles in the world and the use of Indian cotton would both cement Empire links and enable the industry to work again full-time. Both Sam and Boothby represented industrial, largely working-class constituencies and it was after this debate that Churchill singled them out as being among the most promising of the newly elected MPs.

In May Sam spoke in the debate on silk duties and again in June when they came up for discussion during the debate on the Finance Bill. Artificial silk (the first synthetic fibre) was a British invention, but at this time, according to Mr Courtauld writing in the *Manchester Guardian*, it was 'predominantly an ornamental fibre'. Nobody then thought of it as constituting a threat to cotton, although now, in the 1990s, artificial fibres account for the larger part of all textile output in Greater Manchester. Sam said in his speech 'the whole of the artificial silk trade put together is not 1 per cent of the cotton trade'. He supported the proposed imposition of a duty, giving commercial reasons for believing that it would, with rebates for exports, stimulate home production.

He was proud of being an industrialist and set out his ideas in a book, *Industrial Leadership*, which was published in October 1925. Stanley Baldwin wrote the preface. In it Sam expounded his ideas on worker/manager co-operation; the role of the banks and insurance companies in industry; tariffs, finance and the need for some government regulation. Printed under the title were the words: 'He does most who helps his fellow-man to help himself'.

Throughout his life he believed in fostering an enterprising state of mind and sense of personal responsibility. He could not agree with the divisive, class-struggle doctrine of socialism and wrote that your average Britisher, always willing to give a hand, worked for the pleasure and satisfaction of working, as well as for the money. It is not surprising, therefore, that when the welfare state took hold, he was against it. However, he always leaned towards the liberal end of the Conservative spectrum and believed that there should be some state regulation in industrial affairs, particularly in the financial sphere. Like Harold Macmillan (who also entered parliament in 1924), he believed that government had 'to reconcile the need for central direction with the encouragement of individual effort', and when Harold's suggestion for reducing local rates for industry was taken up by Churchill in his 1927 Spring Budget, Sam, speaking in the debate on local government, showed his enthusiasm, saying: 'This will do more to help the cotton trade than any other proposal of which I have heard in recent years.'

Writing at the time when the school-leaving age was under discussion, Sam advocated more industry- and business-oriented education; not so much teaching young people a trade as giving them some understanding of business structure and management. He urged the government to set up trade councils, as Macara had for the cotton industry (abandoned during the war), in which management and employees could discuss their mutual problems. 'The whole outlook of those directing education', he wrote, 'loses sight of the fact that this nation depends upon its industrial prosperity for its very existence. The modern boy or girl,' he complained, 'whether educated in State or Public school, is as difficult to utilise as if no expenditure on education had been made. The curriculum fails to inculcate the primary adjunct to usefulness – the desire to achieve.'

In January 1927, he went to Egypt on a cotton conference, taking Kit with him. Kit asked her father-in-law to 'look after' her three young children while she was away. But instead of reassuring her, John wrote back from Studholme 'your nerves are obviously not good' and advised her to look after her health. (He did not think she ate enough.) Kit was anxious and, before leaving her tall London house, made sure that the escape ladder from the top floor onto the roof was down, in case of fire.

On his return, Sam started working on a scheme for the rationalisation of that portion of Lancashire's cotton-spinning trade that used Egyptian cotton. His contention was that the existing piecemeal, vertical organisation of the mills, where each competed against each, was not conducive to the prosperity of the industry as a whole and prevented it competing successfully with the rest of the world.

He formed a merger committee, of which he was chairman, consisting of ten mill-owners, including himself and his father, who had mills that they were prepared to merge. The results of the proposed reorganisation, they believed, would be: a reduction in production costs, directors' fees, managerial salaries and staff; a stabilisation of prices and savings in operating costs. A detailed report of the proposals was sent to the Bankers Industrial Development Co. Ltd (an agency set up by government to provide finance for such basic industries as cotton), with a copy to the Lord Privy Seal. However, the asked-for loans needed to put the plan into operation were not forthcoming and the government, in spite of having promised an enquiry into the cotton trade, continued to procrastinate.

VII

Finance and Industry

At the time that Sam wrote *Industrial Leadership*, Germany's war debts and reparations were still not settled, in spite of the efforts made at the Brussels Conference of 1920 and the Cannes Conference of 1922, and all the European countries were in debt to the United States. In his speech to the American Bankers Association in New York in November 1922, Reginald McKenna, who in 1915 had been Chancellor of the Exchequer and was now Governor of the Bank of England, warned: 'it is not what the debtors may justly be called upon to pay, *but what they are able to pay*, which we as business men must consider.' Yet in 1925 when Churchill was Chancellor of the Exchequer, he put Britain back on the gold standard at pre-war parity (in spite of McKenna's and Keynes's objections) and money became tighter than ever.

'Industry', wrote Sam in his book, 'has to pay too much for the use of money. Banks are able to obtain a much greater reward by borrowing and lending money than can be obtained from manufacturing industry. The interests of the banker and the manufacturer, instead of running side by side, run in divergent, if not opposite, directions. Financial institutions have gained strength as industry has lost it. Talking Free Trade does not create markets.'

He disagreed with the policy of deflation that had been pursued since 1920. 'When trade is improving and the unemployed are being absorbed into industry,' he wrote, 'if the price level is to remain stable, monetary policy should be directed to an increase in the supply of money.' 'No trade can stand up against a continuing decline in the purchasing power of the public,' he wrote in another article. 'If we mean to get rid of unemployment we must have more money in existence.' He pointed to the USA, where the volume of money was expanding and prosperity was on the increase. But whereas there only 40 per cent of currency was supported by gold here, banks would only give loans, or invest, up to the amount of their cash resources, *not beyond*. 'Increased trade', he wrote, 'calls for more money in circulation because otherwise prices will fall; and ever since the end of the war, prices here have been falling.'

Before Henry Ford's revolutionary ideas had been put into practice and proven right, Sam favoured giving the people greater purchasing power. He wanted to lower the burden of taxation and at the same time impose specific tariffs for specific industries. Finance and industry, he thought, should have the same objectives, and all his life he fought against the stranglehold of banks impeding the expansion of manufacturing. He advocated legislation obliging banks to loan to industry at preferential rates in times of recession, not, as they were doing, demanding ever higher returns. 'It lies within the power of parliament to do this for our country', he said in a speech. 'Business debt is largely due to ill-informed, previous boom lending', he contended. 'If industry has to forgo dividends in bad times, why not banks? Why should banks actually make increased profits at such times?' He also advocated lowering the interest on Government Bonds so that industry should not have to compete against them for funding.

In 1926 Sam became a member of the Industrial Group in the House of Commons and in the following year was made Parliamentary Secretary to the Financial Secretary to the Treasury with his own room in the Treasury, overlooking Horse Guards Parade. *Industrial Leadership* was reprinted and his ideas on the relationship between monetary policy, prosperity and industry began to gain credence.

People on the whole remained optimistic, believing that once the post-war difficulties were overcome, everything would be all right. There were high hopes for the League of Nations, which pledged the world to collective security. Ireland had received (at least partial) independence. The Imperial Conference in London in 1926 had set up independent governments in Canada, Australia and New Zealand, 'the Crown to govern all *only* according to the wishes of each independent parliament'. However, the General Strike, which Sam's brother-in-law, Jeff Wakley, helped to defeat by driving a train, showed that there was still little understanding of working-class conditions among the better off.

The difference in lifestyles between poor and rich is illustrated by the house that Sam took in Princes Gardens when he moved his family to London in the autumn of 1925. It had five floors and a basement. In the latter, Mrs Barrow, the cook, had a full-time scullerymaid to assist her. On the ground floor was a pantry for McKenzie, next to the dining room. In the drawing room, which took up the whole of the first floor and led through to a conservatory full of plants with a little pond in the centre, there was a grand piano with a pianola. The first floor was a bedroom floor, and the floor above was for the children, with Nanny and a nurserymaid. There were three maid's rooms on the fifth floor as well as one where Ruby Hubbard, Kit's personal maid, did all the family sewing. McKenzie valeted for Sam and a secretary came in daily. The chauffeur had his own flat above the garage in the mews. Sam worked in his library on the ground floor, for which he bought a huge kneehole desk and a vast Victorian-Gothic bookcase.

As well as his big London house, he rented a house at Littlestone-on-Sea, Kent, where he took his whole family (and most of his staff) for holidays. He liked driving fast and motored down in his Delage leaving the chauffeur to bring Kit, Nanny and the children in the saloon. The rest of the household came by train. Peter Wakley, Jeff and Eve's son (born 1924), was a regular visitor, staying several weeks each summer, and among the adult weekend guests were two regulars, both student doctors: Stuart Hensman and John Bray. After Hensman qualified and opened a practice in Chester Street, SW1, Sam and Kit became his patients and it was he who was looking after Sam when he died. Bray made an important medical discovery about infantile dysentery, which received acclaim. However, he did not go on to practise medicine, becoming more interested in making money. Sam was to become his mother's adviser and trustee of her estate.

Many of the families who holidayed at Littlestone knew each other from London, and the house Sam rented looked like a small edition of his London one (basement and all) planted incongruously right on the seafront. There was no sea wall (as now) and these basements were often flooded. The lifeboat was launched manually; the need to push it out was heralded by a siren so that all able-bodied men should rush and lend a hand. The chief attraction of the place was golf. There were three courses, all served by the same clubhouse, and the Prince of Wales (later Edward VIII) played there frequently. In May 1927, when Lindbergh flew from New York to Le Bourget, the first ever transatlantic flight, Sam, Kit and their two little daughters were introduced to him and shook hands when the Prince of Wales brought him to the Houses of Parliament, where they were having tea on the terrace.

Sam was in the parliamentary golf team and early in 1928 went to Gleneagles with it in a group that included Robert Boothby and the Macmillans, and they were all photographed for the *Tatler*. Later that year Sam wrote to Kit from Torquay, where his father was convalescing after a chest infection. 'Father is better than I thought. There is a small nine-hole course. We played this afternoon and I think he quite enjoyed it.'

In 1926, with Sam a newly elected MP, he and Kit were

presented at court (Kit by the Duchess of Devonshire). Sam, as an officer of the reserve, was entitled to wear uniform and wrote to the War Office for instructions. However, as no full dress uniform for the Tank Corps had yet been approved and he did not want to go in service dress uniform, he went in court dress, with a sword, a cutaway coat and black knee-breeches. Kit wore a pink satin gown and carried a huge ostrich-feather fan. They came upstairs to the nursery to show themselves off to the children.

Then, as now, much entertaining was done for charitable causes. Lady Newnes (wife of the newspaper owner), who was their neighbour in Princes Gardens, did a lot of it and Kit soon found herself involved. When Lena (Lady Newnes) organised an Egyptian tableau in aid of some hospital, Kit posed in a shoulder-length wig, holding the fly-swat with long golden horsehair and an ivory handle that she had brought back from the cotton conference in Egypt. She also went once a week to the Battersea Mission to do voluntary social work with needy children. There she met Kathleen Watt, wife of the literary agent Bill Watt of A.P. Watt & Sons, and the two women and their children became friends. (One of the Watt girls married one of Walter Wilson's sons.)

Kit would not sleep alone and whenever Sam was in the north on business, or otherwise away, she had her personal maid, Ruby, to sleep with her in her room or, later, one of her daughters. She loved her children and even kept the early letters enclosing their scribbles which were sent to her by Nanny when she and Sam were on holiday in Brittany in 1926. She wrote to them regularly when they were at boarding school and kept all their letters. Sam did not write to them. He made sporadic attempts to instruct them, leaving Penelope (aged seven), when he was away in Germany, with an exercise book into which she was supposed to write 'What I have Learned Today', and attempting to help them with their arithmetic. But he let Kit choose the schools they were to be sent to, giving in to her belief that girls needed a different education from boys.

All his letters were to Kit. Whenever he was away, he wrote to her. In one letter, from Manchester, when he was on constituency business, he wrote that he had made two speeches and played golf with his cousin Cyril. In another he wrote that he had 'danced with two' (at some Stockport function), which must have displeased her because when next he wrote he said that he repented and asked for her forgiveness. In August 1926 he left her at Littlestone to return to London, writing: 'most exciting debate in the House.' He wrote to her again from Manchester in November, when she was staying with the Walter Wilsons. In fact, even if they were only separated for a couple of nights, he would write or send a telegram, although there was a telephone in the Princes Gardens house, as there had been at The Beeches in Cheshire.

For the next four years Sam wrote a regular weekly feature on various political topics for the *Manchester Evening Chronicle*. It was called 'Pen Pictures in Parliament' and was printed with his profile against the traditional view of the Houses of Parliament from across the river. He also, after returning from the cotton conference in Egypt in February 1927, wrote an article on the political situation in that country for the *Stockport Advertiser*. In August, following John Maynard Keynes's talk to leaders of the Lancashire cotton trade, *The Economist* published an article by Sam on Cotton Mill Finance, in which he made proposals for converting borrowed money into shares. In November *The Graphic* printed his article 'Towards a Nation of Capitalists' and another appeared in the *Textile Mercury*, entitled 'Relation of Finance & Production', the latter journal citing him as 'Man of the Moment' in both 1927 and 1928.

Also in 1928 he wrote an article in *The Banker* in connection with the committee that the government had set up under the chairmanship of Lord Macmillan, an eminent lawyer, to enquire into finance and industry. Reginald MacKenna and John Maynard Keynes both sat on it, so did Ernest Bevin; yet the gold standard was not discussed or questioned and only Ernest Bevin believed that it was doomed.

In May Sam spoke in the debate on currency and banknotes, when the issuing powers of the Bank of England were under consideration and the fiduciary issue rounded up, and in October he was made Chairman of the Parliamentary Commercial Committee and went to Germany with it for an inter-parliamentary conference.

In a trading climate of very tight money everybody was praising free trade, yet each country, led by the USA, was imposing tariff barriers to defend itself against cheap imports. Sam wrote a long article in the *Manchester Guardian* on the gold standard and later the same year he had his picture drawn for the *Financial News* by Ginsburg.

His vulcanised-fibre business, S. Noton & Sons, which his father had bought for him on his marriage, was doing well. Besides making canisters for the cotton trade, it had now started to make luggage. Sam was ambitious to expand it and negotiated an amalgamation with two other luggage-making firms to found S. Noton Ltd. Each of the amalgamating firms contributed directors: Israel Gold, Coleman Sharp and Joseph Rachow from the Attaché Case Co., Philip Dix and Max Wolsey from The Suit Case Manufacturing Co. and Sam and Cyril Hammersley from S. Noton & Sons. Sam became Managing Director of the new firm. By the 1940s each of these directors, most of whom were a good deal older than Sam, had resigned, including eventually his cousin Cyril; but one of them, Max Wolsey, stayed with S. Noton Ltd until his retirement a couple of years before Sam's death. In Sam's own words 'the chief business of the company became the manufacture of inexpensive fibre suitcases in competition with continental imports.' Its main factory and registered offices went to Walthamstow in London, but Goddard Street, Oldham, which continued to make canisters for the cotton trade, was retained.

VIII

Economics

Speaking in a debate in parliament on the cotton industry in April 1928, Sam drew the attention of the House to the fact that in Lancashire there were some 60 million spindles, almost a quarter of all those in the world (one for each inhabitant of the United Kingdom). 'The industry,' he said, 'was in very bad straights.' Demands were being made on workers to hold wages and increase hours but mills were not working full-time. This, he explained, was due to the inability to export at competitive prices. Costs were high, partly due to old-fashioned working practices, partly to lack of co-operation between the various sections of the trade and partly to indebtedness to the banks. Earlier he had asked the Chancellor of the Exchequer whether he would consider the introduction of such amendments to the Finance Act, 1927, as to enable existing firms engaged in the cotton-spinning trade to amalgamate without payment of capital and transfer duties, pointing out that 60 per cent of cotton goods from Lancashire were exported.

There was much talk of speculation and profit-taking during the debate, during which T. Shaw said: 'While the Lancashire employer is hard as nails, once his word has passed, the workers know that that word will be honoured.' Sam raised a laugh by offering to *give away* up to 20 mills, debts and all, knowing that the offer would not be accepted.

By 1929 he was submitting two different schemes to the Federation of Master Cotton Spinners Association, one for the amalgamation of 155 cotton-spinning companies and another for forming a merger company for the amalgamation of a small number of 'better class' mills, among which were to be the Delta, Devon, Fern, Manor, Rugby and Atlas mills. In the *Cotton Spinners of the World Directory* for 1928–29 Sam was listed as a Director of the Devon, Fern and Rex mills and his father as Director, or Chairman, of the Lily, Atlas, Belgrave, Delta, Devon, Fernhurst, Manor, Royal, Soudan, Rome, Royd and Rugby mills as well as of the Guidebridge Spinning Co. and the Whitelands Twist Co. An article about Sam headed 'Mr Hammersley's Mill Merger Scheme' appeared in the *Evening Chronicle*. He also had his picture in the *Evening Standard* (and the *Liverpool Post & Mercury*) with the caption: 'S.S. Hammersley MP who is responsible for the Lancashire cotton amalgamation scheme now being drafted in detail by the Federation of Master Cotton Spinners Association.'

In the early months of 1929, he wrote to Kit from Stockport (enclosing an appeal for The Poor Children's Clog Fund) in which he wrote: 'all my meetings have gone off very well. Three on Monday and one big one at Duckenfield tonight. Tomorrow I have two more – Heaton Moor and Hope Hill – then home.' But three days later he sent another letter saying: 'more Stockport speeches to be made.'

For the 1929 general election he rented a house at Knutsford so that the family could be together for the full three weeks of the campaign. It was May and bluebells were out everywhere. The children had matching blue coats and cloche hats and were photographed with their parents by the local press. Gracie Fields was now famous and Sam played her latest songs on the wind-up gramophone. But to please Kit, while he was getting dressed in the mornings and she was having her breakfast in bed, he put on something romantic, like: *Can't help loving that man o' mine* and *Why do I love you?*' He was returned again for Stockport. McKenzie, encouraged by the excited children, helped the gardener make a bluebell arch over the front gate and the whole household turned out to welcome him home after the poll. But, although Sam got in again for Stockport, the Conservatives under Stanley Baldwin were defeated.

In July 1929, when Sam spoke in the debate on the Address at the start of Ramsay MacDonald's government (the first in which women had the vote) he said that 'stimulation of depressed export trades was the crux of the unemployment problem and that increased production could not be applied unless we called a halt to the process of deflation.' During this time he was chairing a conference of representatives from 20 different industries, whose conclusions led to the *Producers Economic Survey*. It was this survey that was largely responsible for the setting up of the Committee of Finance and Industry by Philip Snowdon.

Speaking on 7 October at the luncheon at which the *Producers Economic Survey* was launched, Sam said:

Today there is released for publication an economic memorandum which was sent to the Prime Minister and the Chancellor of the Exchequer last week. The memorandum is the outcome of many meetings held during the last nine months by the representatives of the chief organisations of the producing industries. It reflects the common anxiety shared by agricultural and producing trades that our existing credit structure is not adapted to find a remedy for the special difficulties which beset us.

The fundamental governing characteristic of our national position is well known though its overwhelming importance is not sufficiently appreciated. *The cost of production per unit of goods produced in this country is too high.* This is the basic fact which finds its expression in our inability to create adequate foreign balances abroad, in the weakness of our rates of exchange and in the consequent loss of the essential gold on which our credit it based. If our main producing industries could reduce their costs to a competitive level there would be no necessity to use the instrument of the Bank Rate in order to protect our gold reserves.

Amidst a welter of theories about work, wages and production, one fact shines out like a beacon. It is the tremendous economies which can be effected in the cost of production per unit by means of mass production. Not the low cost of raw materials, not low labour charges but the great saving of large-scale production, is the reason for the domination of the motor-car markets of the world by the United States of America. It is because they make so many motor-cars and enjoy the economies of mass-production that they can provide a high standard of living for the workers as well as a low priced article for the consumer ...

It follows, therefore, that the most practical way to reduce the industrial costs level without attacking our standard of living, is to increase the volume of our production. But if the basic industries of this country are to operate on an increased volume of production, an increase in the amount of credit available will be necessary. *It is precisely at this point that we find that our industrial necessities are in direct opposition to the working of our monetary system.'* On the one hand, modern industrialism indicates that the only sound remedy for high costs involves an increase in the volume of credit, on the other hand the working of our monetary mechanism is such that a high cost level finds its reflection in a decrease in the volume of credit. The signatories of our memorandum welcome the announcement of the Chancellor of the Exchequer that this conflict of interests is to be the subject of an exhaustive enquiry.

There was, however, one indication in the recent speech of the Chancellor which representatives of the

51

producing industries will, in my opinion, view with the deepest apprehension. Mr Snowdon suggested that we may find a solution of our difficulties through a new international bank.

He then proceeded to speak about the *Bank of International Settlements* which, he said, had received very little public comment probably because its indicated scope was so vague that economists as well as industrialists were chary of expressing an opinion on it. It was to be called into existence in order to economise in the use of gold. It will be an international central bank for national central banks.

The factors which make our production non-competitive in comparison with the foreigner are mainly national factors; rates, taxes, wages, hours of labour, insurances, pensions and so forth, which are all nationally controlled. It is impossible to contemplate with equanimity a state of affairs in which the producers' overhead costs will be controlled by the national parliament but his ability to meet these overhead costs will be affected by the policy of an international institution. The present proposals mean nothing less than that the economic life of Europe is to be intrusted to twenty four expert bankers. These bankers will not be susceptible to public opinion. They will not be elected by any democratic mandate. Though nominally representatives of a particular state, they will not be expected to act as though they owed allegiance to any special country. Twenty four economic experts nominated are to form an institution – more powerful than the states that brought it into being – an institution which will have the power in economic matters to override the will of Parliament. If such a state of affairs should come to pass the doom of British basic producing trade will have been sealed. We are, as is well known, essentially a nation of producers. Our production is regulated by every kind of national restriction. If we take away from the nation the right, whenever it may think fit, to adopt a national monetary policy we shall deprive our people of a necessary weapon of defence and may be leave our industries bound and helpless before their competitors. I have said enough to show that the functions of the proposed Bank of International Settlements must be most carefully scrutinised not only by our economic experts but by our industrial leaders. Government by parliament may not be an ideal system but it is certainly infinitely preferable to concealed government by an oligarchy of international financial experts ... Our Committee is asking that our monetary policy shall be determined by a consideration of our needs as a producing nation and not by the dictates of international finance.

But although the Labour Chancellor, Philip Snowdon, set up the promised enquiry (The Committee of Finance and Industry) when he presented his next budget in March 1930 it was clear that there was no change in government economic policy. Sam spoke in the debate on the budget proposals, saying that the extra taxation proposed (£44 million) would only further reduce money available for investment in the basic industries whose rationalisation it was Labour's avowed policy to pursue. And in this same debate he again talked about the need for industrial rationalisation and modernisation, particularly in the cotton industry, and again he stressed the need for financial help from the Government.

There was much talk of amalgamation but the only practical proposals for amalgamation before the Lancashire people were the proposals of the Lancashire Cotton Corporation which operated by calling in the capital of financially-embarrassed units, thus ruining small shareholders. They could force amalgamations as they alone were supported by the Bank of England and the Joint Stock Banks in the North and already they were proposing amalgamations with the Egyptian section of the trade, which was profit-making. However, on the same Bank of England basis of four shillings per spindle, when the cost of replacement was fifty shillings, such amalgamations were not acceptable. No mills could rationalise and make independent amalgamations without finance and the finance was blocked to them because it was only available through the Lancashire Cotton Corporation.

He condemned the Labour Party for doing nothing, in spite of its election promises, but only succeeded in provoking the next speaker (Labour) into saying that what he (Sam) had said: 'showed above all a failure of capitalism'. Yet Sam returned to the subject again when he spoke in the debate on the address to the King's Speech in October 1930 (the time of the R101 airship disaster).

'Sixteen months ago' he said, 'the Government had stated that it had plans to deal effectively with unemployment. That it had not was because the great industrial problem of how to rationalise and reorganise our basic industries seems to have been evaded; and the two were inevitably, linked ... The cotton trade,' he went on: 'has the responsibility of providing a livelihood for two million people. Yet during the time the Enquiry (the Committee of Finance & Industry) has been running; and it started to work two years ago; exports of cotton yarn have been reduced by approximately one third and cotton cloth exports by nearly a half. Where previously two men had been unemployed there were now three and where one woman had been unemployed before, there were now two.'

He savaged the Enquiry's report, saying that its recommen-

dations were well known to the industry before it began
and that their report was a collection of innocuous industrial aphorisms, a symposium of copy-book maxims.
Neither did he have a good word to say for the government's other attempt to help the cotton industry: The
Bankers Industrial Development Co. This, he contended,
was not a suitable arbiter of finance for the industry
because it was not impartial. Far from putting Lancashire
in touch with the City (as promised) it was more interested
in salvaging a collection of bankrupt units, which it had
bought cheaply through the Lancashire Cotton Corporation.

> I say that, within my own knowledge, it is impossible
> for efficient concerns to go to the many financial
> houses which exist in the City of London and discuss
> with them any questions of cotton finance because the
> answer that they get is that the Bankers Industrial
> Development Co. deals with that; you must go there.
> ... I want to make what I consider a practical and
> helpful suggestion, namely that the government set up
> an impartial, new body to contain representatives of
> the joint stock banks, of the industry and possibly of
> government.

His speech was strongly supported by Dr. A.V. Davies, the
member for Royton (another cotton-spinning constituency)
who followed him. Then, when the Under Secretary to the
Board of Trade, winding up the debate, justified the
government by saying that it had provided the Bankers
Industrial Development Co. with £6 million Sam spoke
again, protesting that no new money had come in the
direction of viable Lancashire firms but that all of it had
gone to the Lancashire Cotton Corporation, of which he
had spoken earlier. 'The case is,' he said, 'that the government set up the Bankers Industrial Development Co. as a
means whereby the State could be brought into touch with
industry but they had abrogated their functions to this

body and I am making criticisms in respect of the way in which that body is performing that function. The Hon. gentleman,' he concluded, 'has not answered that point at all.'

He intervened in several debates later that year, asking questions on the cotton trade, unemployment and the economic situation. In the Unemployment Insurance Bill debate he said that, while approving of the extra money being allocated to the fund, he could not see that it would do anything to provide jobs. The Parliamentary Secretary to the Minister of Labour had said 'Find the men work and they will readily take it.' 'But,' said Sam, 'I say to the Labour Government, pursue a policy which will enable people to provide work, and then you will deal with the problem.'

In a further debate on unemployment a week later, he repeated many of the arguments he had put forward earlier about the position of Britain's basic industries. 'Industry's profits', he said, 'are not directed now towards keeping itself up to date but towards paying interest on debt. There had been a transference of wealth from the pockets of the active sections of the community into the pockets of the non-producers. There are two ways,' he went on, 'to reduce unemployment – increase productivity and reduce the burden of debt on industry. The world is not suffering from over-production but from under consumption.'

It may well have been this speech to which Lord Coleraine (born Richard Law) referred in his memoirs (uncompleted) when he wrote that, before he became an MP, he had listened to a speech by Sam which particularly impressed him. 'Sam Hammersley,' he wrote, 'had forgotten more about the cotton industry than the appropriate department of the Board of Trade ever knew. It was he who stirred in my mind vague and indeterminate thoughts about the possibility of stimulating consumption rather than restricting production.'

Richard Law, who was to hold ministerial posts under Churchill, was the youngest of the four sons (two had been

56

killed in the First World War) of the late Prime Minister, Andrew Bonar Law. By his own admission, he did not at this time know much about either industry or finance. He was a journalist and in 1930 published a letter in *The Spectator*, which read: Some form of regulation of industry is almost certainly inevitable and even desirable and capitalism, if it is to retrieve its more obvious failures, may be compelled to borrow freely of socialist theory.

In his memoirs, written nearly half a century later, he declares this to have been an absurd idea, dismissing his own early 'radical' leanings as the inexperience of youth. But at the time he wrote it he was a frequent visitor to Princes Gardens where he and Sam paced up and down Sam's library late into the night, often with Norman Crump of *The Economist*, trying to put the world to rights. At that time, like Sam and Harold Macmillan, Law felt that laissez-faire capitalism alone was not enough and that new ideas were needed to create a fairer and more stable society with less human waste. It was only later that he became a true-blue Tory, whereas both Sam and Harold Macmillan retained their belief in the need for some 'socialist' measures, even though they criticised the excesses of the welfare state.

IX

Monetary Policy

By 1930 Sam could no longer afford to live at Princes
Gardens and his house in Littlestone. Giving them both
up, he moved to the country, where he rented Stroods, a
house on Lord Rankeillour's estate near Uckfield in
Sussex. Richard Law, who had previously only visited
Sam for late-night political discussions, now introduced
Mary, his American-born wife, and both became frequent
weekend guests. He wrote later in his memoirs that it was
at this time that 'Sam Hammersley, his wife and family,
became and remained our very close and much loved
friends.'   Both Dick and Sam were now prospective
fathers, as Mary was expecting her first child and Kit her
fourth. They enjoyed making jokes, particularly about
pregnant women, but they also had serious discussions
concerning the economic depression following the collapse
of world markets.
   Both basically believed in free trade but Dick, like Max
Beaverbrook, with whom the Law children had lived after
the death of their father, argued for Empire preference
while Sam wanted protection for British exports. In the
financial field both of them supported Keynes, although
even in the spring of 1931, when the revised budget
proposals were discussed, Keynes was not yet advocating
the abandonment of the gold standard but only talking of
the restraints it put on British banks to maintain liquidity.
   Sam had a number of Keynes's books, including *Essays
in Persuasion*, given to him for Christmas 1931 by the poet
Edward Shanks, who was married to Kit's cousin.

Maynard Keynes had impressed him ever since accepting the invitation of the Federation of Master Cotton Spinners Association to come and give them his opinions on reorganisation back in 1927. Keynes's belief that banks were parasites on industry echoed Sam's own thoughts. He had also told the Master Cotton Spinners that, in times of contraction, it was important to concentrate production in the hands of the most efficient units, which was what Sam was constantly trying to get across to the Bankers Industrial Development Company, whose money was going to supporting the lame ducks of the Lancashire Cotton Corporation.

On 15 September 1931 he spoke in the House of Commons on the Revised Budget Proposals. Quoting the words of the 1930 International Bankers' Committee in respect of the money that London had lent to Germany, he said:

There is no doubt that the short-term credits to German banks have to a very large extent been used in the internal economy [of Germany] as working capital and therefore cannot be readily withdrawn without grave damage to the financial structure. The position is that money which British banks properly considered, in the light of all financial rectitude, could not be lent to British industries, was lent to German bankers and therefore to German industries ...

The abnormally vulnerable condition of the City is well known and was commented upon by the Macmillan Committee nearly two years ago ... The crisis is a crisis of deflation, a shortage of money or lack of credit. As a practical person engaged in our largest export industry I want to lay as much emphasis on this as possible. It has not only directly added to the burden of debt and increased overhead costs in this country but it has prevented us having the available capital to reconstruct and re-equip industry. What steps are being taken? We are balancing the budget by

59

increased taxation and cuts in expenditure – there is nothing in the budget that will help the trade situation. The delusion of the City of London has been the belief that in looking after itself it has been looking after the country. We have to support the government because it is in a hole. But I hope we will soon have another government, a party pledged to consider the producers of this country, a party pledged to put the producers first and not last in our national affairs. It is only by putting the producers first that the pound will be safe.

But when at last Britain came off the gold standard and a national government with MacDonald and Baldwin as joint Prime Ministers was formed, the country was still faced with apparently insoluble problems. Britain was still owed as much by Germany and her late allies as she owed to the United States, and all European economies were bedevilled by unsettled war debts. But Sam warned that the economy campaign which the new government initiated (and which Keynes thought folly) was only going to make things worse.

The Sixth Assembly of the League of Nations set up a preparatory committee, on which 21 nations were represented, which came up with a very good and detailed diagnosis of world economic conditions. Their figures showed that between 1929 and 1932 the volume of world trade fell by approximately one-quarter. But solutions were not forthcoming because the delegates had no powers and did not represent their respective governments, which, in any case, were not prepared to relinquish their economic nationalism.

During 1931 Sam wrote two articles in the *Stockport Advertiser*, one entitled: 'Off the Gold Standard' and the other 'Economic Crisis'. In a speech he made in the House in February urging support for the cotton industry, he said: 'Working-class rents must be reduced for us to get back to competitive production,' pointing out that these were 54 per cent higher than in 1914. But it was not only for 'competitive production' that he wanted rents reduced; he also had in mind the disproportionate profits of the landlords and the danger of letting in Communism because of lowered living standards.

He asked a question in the House in support of one asked by Earl Castle Stewart about the stabilisation of silver, which was vital in assuring the financial credit of India. Sam was now Arthur Castle Stewart's neighbour as well as Harold Macmillan's and, meeting in each other's houses while their children partied, they had serious discussions on monetary matters and the Depression.

When Sam spoke in March about Indian tariffs being imposed against British cotton goods, he agreed that the people of India had to be protected. 'But,' he said, 'these tariffs protect the rich mill-owners not the poor consumers and they do this at the expense of our own people.' He gave figures to show that the cost of producing cotton goods in India had decreased over the last ten years whereas the selling price had increased. So who, he asked, were the tariffs protecting?

In July he asked a question of the PM on the proposed credit to the Government of India 'in view of his refusal to use British credit to reorganise British industries' and four more questions on financial assistance to trade with India. On 9 July he made a speech in which he complained that the government was turning a blind eye to the continued boycotting of British goods by India, instigated by the Congress Party's civil disobedience campaign. 'From two of my own mills,' he said, 'one with 100,000 spindles and the other with 200,000 spindles, where previously every pound of yarn went to India, now not one ounce was sent.' He then followed up his questions on silver by saying that it was in the power of the Government of India to control the selling of silver, which was keeping prices down both here and in India, and causing uncertainty in world markets.

In January 1932 he gave a talk to the British Association

of Managers of Textile Works on the subject of Great Britain's national debt problems. 'There is this phenomenal increase in real wealth,' he said, 'and side by side with it there is unemployment and serious poverty. Why is it?' It was, he suggested, because the means of exchange had become inadequate; money, which was the link between production and consumption, was not fulfilling its proper purpose. He then quoted the moderate return on investment received prior to 1914, saying that, thanks to the deflationary policy of the government since 1920 together with its priority in maintaining gold reserves, a disproportionately high rate of interest now obtained. 'The only conclusion one can come to in examining the altered state of affairs is that today the rentier is extracting too much from the economic system. You cannot carry on the economic system for a long period of years unless industry makes a profit.'

He then went on to speak about reparations and compared the millions that were being spent to rebuild German industry with the way British industry was being starved of funds through the policy of high interest rates being pursued by British bankers and the Treasury. They did this, he said, 'in order to protect gold reserves. But the most desirable way to protect gold reserves is through the establishment of foreign credits by the sale of goods. We in this country have never looked to the industrial method of dealing with our financial problem.' Speaking of the possibility of excusing Germany her reparations payments, which, he said, was a policy 'strongly advocated by financial interests in London and finding its echo in the British Treasury', he protested that British industry would then be left to find the £55 million a year, *unless* we repudiate our debt to America; and this he did not think would be honourable. The British people, he said, were not being property informed of the alternatives. 'As a country we still suffer from the Victorian inhibition of not being candid about our means. British industry,' he insisted, 'must be helped to become credit-worthy. This practical aim of endeavouring to make the basic trades credit-worthy seems to me to be entirely overlooked. Those people who control our financial policy seem to direct their energies to make the world safe for bankers. A world safe for bankers,' he concluded, 'is the greatest illusion of this age.'

However, there were some faint signs of recovery in Britain during 1932, although few in the rest of the world. Sam's financial position improved enough for him to be able to write to McKenzie, who had kept in touch with the family since they left London, prompting her to reply that she would be pleased to have her old job back. The Sunday ritual of singing *A Little Bit Off the Top* when she brought the joint into the dining room was renewed now at Stroods, much to the delight of the children. In the United States, however, Hoover failed to deal with the economic crisis and was defeated by Roosevelt, prompting Keynes to advocate a public works programme for Britain on the lines of the New Deal. Dick Law came back from a visit to America singing *Buddy, Can You Spare a Dime?* But the government was frightened of inflation and continued with its restrictive policies.

In March 1933, speaking in the Budget debate, Sam proposed a two-part motion (seconded by Leo Amery) welcoming the government's declared intention to raise wholesale prices, which was reported in both *The Economist* and the *Evening Standard*. 'Such a rise,' he argued, 'should only cause a small rise in retail prices and an even smaller one in the cost of living and this would be greatly outweighed by increased employment and profitable production. In 1924,' he said, 'the wholesale price level was more than 60 per cent higher than today and we had less than half as many unemployed. The increase in unemployment in every part of the world, accompanied by a decline in production, can in the main be attributed to the fall in the level of prices. Such a situation disadvantages that part of the population that can produce wealth, employer and employee alike, while benefiting those on fixed incomes.'

He then went on to say that he did not agree with the findings of the Macmillan Committee (which had reported in 1931) that the way to raise these prices was by co-operation through an international conference. Such a conference, even if it worked, would put Britain at a disadvantage because, he said: 'when Britain returned to the Gold Standard at pre-war parity the pound was already over-valued; what was needed was to devalue it.' Government strategy, he maintained, had been directed to bolstering up a dear pound instead of looking to the efficiency and productive capacity of our main basic industries.

The second part of his motion was that the government, without waiting for international co-operation, should go for an expansive monetary policy and increase the amount of money in circulation. 'But,' he said, 'we cannot force bankers to lend if they consider it unsafe to lend, or people to borrow if they do not see a profitable use for increased funds.' He proposed subsidies for selected exports to make basic industries more credit-worthy from the point of view of bankers; government expenditure on works of national importance; and reduction of taxes. 'Confidence is the life-blood of trade,' he said; 'the probability of higher prices is confidence.' The motion was carried.

He spoke again in May and July of that same year, pressing for cheap money and government investment in industry and complaining that 'our export industries are taxed more highly than anywhere else in the world,' and was so persistent that Hore Belisha, replying for the government, said tartly: 'the views which my Hon. Friend so frequently expresses have been noted.'

Sam, however, continued to speak out on the issues that he was well-placed to know about and which he considered important. A question he asked about the cotton trade showed that the government was negotiating tariffs with Japan without consulting the Federation of Master Cotton Spinners Association, thus Lancashire was not speaking with one voice, as he believed it should. It appeared from the *Board of Trade Journal* that between 1932 and 1933 Japanese trade had increased both in volume and value, while Lancashire's had declined.

To quote from Lord Coleraine's memoirs again:

> I could never understand why Sam's parliamentary career was relatively such a minor one. He was a good speaker who knew his subject. But he suffered from a severe handicap: he was actively engaged in industry, and it was one of the myths of the Baldwin era (which Baldwin himself despite his own business background rather encouraged than otherwise) that any Member of Parliament with industrial interests must be there to feather his own nest. It never seemed to occur to anybody that he might have specialised knowledge which, thrown into the common pool, would have added to it.

X

India

Besides the suspicion of industrialists which Lord Coleraine wrote about, Sam was handicapped in the Conservative Party of his time by not having been to a public school. He also held a left-of-centre position, analogous to that of Tory-Democrat or Radical, to which Robert Boothby attributed his own failure to be offered high office, and, like Boothby, he had an affair with another Member of Parliament's wife.

Stockport returned two members, and in the 1931 general election Sam was joined there by Alan Dower (also a Conservative). Sam had known him for some time and Kit and Alan's wife Lavender had at first been good friends with a mutual interest in interior decoration. When the Hammersleys still lived at Princes Gardens, Kit had helped Lavender paint a bathroom in her Lowndes Square house with a ceiling of moon and stars. Yet even before Alan joined Sam in Stockport, Kit was referring to her as 'the cat' or 'the creature'. Across a letter full of phrases such as 'my little wife' and 'my dearest, best, most beautiful', which she received from Sam while she was at Stroods, awaiting her fourth child, Kit scribbled: 'could one believe there was such base treachery as this – written at the time you kissed her!' The affair cost Sam his seat; yet Lavender was made godmother to the new baby, a fourth daughter, (Jenniver Mary Œnone) who was christened in the Crypt of the House of Commons, with Stanley Baldwin's son Oliver as the godfather.

Kit talked about divorce, in spite of Sam's assurances

that she was his only love, and there were terrible shouting matches between them, ending in her turning him out of the house. He stayed with Jeff and Eve Wakley while Jeff tried to get his sister to forgive him and to take him back. Kit agreed, on condition that he gave up Stockport and swore a solemn oath that he would never look at another woman again. She kept the paper with this 'oath' all her life. It was accompanied by a financial penalty and witnessed by E.M. Poulton (Nanny). To seal their reconciliation, in January 1932 they went to Scotland for a holiday and their picture with the caption 'Wintersporting at Braemar' appeared in the *Tatler*.

In his resignation speech announcing that he did not intend to contest Stockport again (a decision which was reported in the Manchester papers) Sam said: 'it is clear to me that my Conservatism and Dower's are incompatible.' (In an early 1930 letter to Kit, he had written: 'I feel myself less and less in sympathy with orthodox Conservatism'). But, ironically, Alan also resigned, complaining that Sam did not co-operate with him in the constituency and that the agent was working more for Sam than he was for him.

In the spring of 1933 Sam's father died. He caught pneumonia after sleeping out of doors, which was something he loved to do but which his daughter Gladys begged him not to. Sam knew that he had been worried about his various cotton-spinning businesses which had been losing money (the Atlas Mill was liquidated in 1930) but it was only after his father died that he discovered the extent of the mess his affairs were in. Account books, written up neatly by hand, showed annual increases in his assets from 1906 to 1920 and thereafter losses, each year, of several thousand pounds. He had loan books and interest on shares from 26 different mills but the sums were derisory. He left a copy of a letter to one of his creditors, dated August 1932 (handwritten in an exercise book with a carbon) asking for cash payments instead of payments into his bank. Years before he had had to mortgage, or forfeit, titles he owned to land, shops and premises in the centre of Oldham. Always an optimist, he died overwhelmed by affairs he knew he could no longer control.

Sam went up to Lancashire. As executor of his father's will, he was worried about the many 'calls' against the estate and particularly wanted to protect Gladys. Both his sisters believed that he had only resigned from Stockport in order to be able to deal with his father's affairs, and their children all believed it too. When he returned to Stroods he brought Gladys back with him and she stayed for several weeks.

In the autumn he left for India on a textile mission, on which he represented the Federation of Master Cotton Spinners Association. Since March 1930 he had been asking questions in the House about India's imposition of tariffs on cotton piece-goods from Britain. He did not feel that the Secretary of State for India (Leo Amery) was standing up strongly enough for the interests of Lancashire and it was important that the vexed question of trade in cotton goods between Britain and India be settled.

Before going to India he wrote several articles in the *Stockport Advertiser* on the danger of cheap imports of cotton goods from the East, including one entitled 'The Yellow Peril'. He spoke in a debate in the House, calling on the government to protect the Empire from being flooded with cheap Japanese textiles, and, a couple of weeks later, spoke of Ceylon's failure to comply fully with the terms of the Ottawa Agreement on Empire trade. He reminded the House that, under Ceylon's constitution the Governor-General could overrule the Council of State in questions of paramount importance, saying that he considered the present trade war to be such a question.

Although the Government of India Act of 1919 had given elected representatives of the people a share in the government (in practice, two-thirds of the seats) and had made reforms in the powers of provincial legislative councils, the Indian Nationalists were not satisfied. In 1920 Gandhi had announced that he would not co-operate with the British, and the repression of 'extremists' followed. Thus Sam and his delegation came up against a powerful faction which aimed to disrupt all and any attempts at further British–Indian co-operation.

He wrote to Kit almost every day, both from the ship and after he landed, long 13- and 15-page lovesick letters, and when he did not hear from her for several days, he was desperate. 'I wish I could do more to please you', he wrote. 'Because I have been an idiot on one occasion is all the more reason why I should never do it again. I never shall.' Once arrived in Bombay, he wrote her long letters from the Taj Mahal Hotel, telling her about the progress of the negotiations. In one he wrote: 'the mill-owners are by no means united. Everyone is intriguing against everyone else.' And in another: 'the Japs gave a party as a display of strength', followed by 'I played golf with the Japanese Consul – a diplomatic gesture'. Then a few days later: 'sweated blood in the preparation of a memo for the Government of India advocating the removal of the specific duty on yarn.'

He found the heat difficult to bear, complaining of the smell of sweat. The British delegation had hoped that they and the Indians would submit a joint report to the Indian Government before the conference in Simla, but this did not happen; each submitted a separate memo. 'The Japs are hopeless,' he wrote, 'the Indians have already broken with them.'

Kit's letters to him were full of how much she was missing him, mentioning the Ichthyboskoi whom Sam had left to look after her while he was away. But she did not trust him. 'I think of you every evening dressing for dinner, going down to dinner, spying out the woman you want to talk to and determinedly seeking her out and dancing with her and sitting out on deck with her or leaning on the rails looking at the moon on the water', she wrote. She was also feeling insecure, afraid that she had changed, that she was ugly and he would not like her when he got home. 'I am very lonely without you.'

In one of his letters Sam begs her to carry out some constituency duties in his absence: 'Do it for my sake.' She answered him, writing that she was learning her speech and had asked Norman Crump a question about the New Deal for inclusion in it and 'received pages of information from *The Economist* and a tome of a letter – much too difficult!' In the next letter she wrote: 'Stockport grey and depressing. Speech not too bad but "the creature" about. Stayed with the Dehns and tossed and turned thinking how badly you had let us both down.'

The letters alternated between affection and suspicion. 'I should never have let you go', she wrote in one, and 'your letters are a joy and comfort', in another. She wrote that 'Bags' (his sister Gladys) had come for the weekend with her daughter Joan (later called Joanna) and that Jeff and Eve had been the next weekend. In the following letter she wrote about getting the two eldest girls off to boarding school; Barbara Jill's sticking-out teeth were going to have to be regulated. But, after she had gone again to Stockport to propose some vote of thanks in his constituency, her letter begged: 'I cannot carry on alone; come home.' Then, in a happier mood, she wrote that she had stayed with Lallie Lee and Geoffrey Lowis at their London house and gone with them to see Marlene Dietrich's latest film. Geoffrey Lowis was a stockbroker on the Naval Reserve. He was small, dark and wiry and had made a lot of money from Eagle Star, which he invested in Matthew Smith paintings; he was also a member of Crockford's and a very good bridge player. His American-born wife was large and fair and pleasure-loving. Both were close friends with Sam and Kit.

Sam was now in Simla, at the Hotel Cecil, very impressed by the grandeur of the scenery, the snow-capped mountain peaks in the distance and the lush greens. Towards the end of the conference he wrote (referring to the Indians): 'with a little accommodation from them we could effect an arrangement of great mutual value.' But the next day everything was going wrong. 'The success of the delegation is balancing on the point of a needle', he wrote. 'The Indians have been trying to squeeze us but we are standing fast. Now it is their turn to feel afraid of a breakdown.'

He wrote her a letter for her birthday, 22 October, addressed to 'The most beautiful Lady in the World' from 'Your unworthy knight – your loving and devoted husband – your eternally constant lover.' Then, at last, he wrote: 'We have brought it off – an agreement with the Bombay mill-owners!' It has not been easy; the Amedabad people have done their damnedest to wreck the whole thing.' (Amedabad was the centre from which Gandhi drew most of his support.) The Indian press had headlines like 'A Betrayal of India', 'An Infamous Agreement' and 'A Humiliating Surrender'. But the Lancashire men had got what they wanted and Sam was coming home. He wired for Kit to meet him at the Ritz.

On his return from India, he wrote an article for the *Stockport Advertiser* on 'Saving Our Trade with India' and the *Journal of the East India Association* published his pamphlet 'The Lancashire Textile Mission to India', which was the basis for his article in the *Evening Chronicle* 'India Must be Our Ally'.

He continued to take an interest in India, supporting Lord Derby when Churchill brought a breach of privilege charge against him in 1934 (not substantiated) in connection with the Indian tariff arrangements. During February 1935 he asked four separate questions in the House about Britain's trade with India in cotton and about the India–Burma trade agreement. In July, in his capacity as chairman of Lancashire MPs, he wrote to Lord Derby and received a handwritten letter in reply. 'I am more pleased than I can say,' Derby wrote, 'to get your resolution and I thank the members most sincerely and I want myself to thank you personally for the way in which you have backed me up in what was for both of us a very difficult situation.' In March 1936 he invited Sam to a dinner which he gave for Lord Linlithgow, Viceroy designate, before the latter left for India.

The Lancashire cotton trade continued to decline. When Sam had asked a question in the House about wages levels (before he went to India) he received the reply (written) that the average level of full-time weekly wages in 1932 had been 4 per cent lower than in 1924. Lancashire, however, kept trying. In October 1934 the Federation of Master Cotton Spinners Association agreed a redundancy scheme (like 'scrap and build' in shipping) under which 10 million spindles were to be scrapped (or sealed). But they could not get the whole industry to agree and the plan was not implemented. Sam asked questions in the House about Japanese exports to Empire countries, particularly West Africa, that were undercutting Lancashire and he complained generally about competition from the Far East. He also told the House that Australia was putting high tariffs against British cotton goods and that Iraq was in breach of a treaty agreement by ordering uniforms and other textile stores from Japan.

'By imposing tariffs we are trying to establish scarcity,' he said, speaking during the second reading of the Finance Bill for the 1932 Budget in which many new tariffs were proposed. 'We have improved scientific knowledge, increased mechanical power and increased natural resources but we find ourselves trying to cheat the prolific quality of nature by imposing restrictions.' Then, moving from the theoretical sphere of what was desirable to the more restricted sphere of the practically attainable, he went on to say:

When we came off the Gold Standard and devalued, international capital rushed to this country. The exchange value of our currency has gone up higher than the value justified by the profit-earning capacity of the country. This has been followed very quickly by a drop in trade and further unemployment. The price of the pound and the value of British Government securities will look after themselves if we adopt a policy to help industry. It is within the government's power to raise prices within the sterling area by increasing credit. The ultimate value of the pound depends on our ability to import raw materials and foodstuffs and to pay for them by the export of manufactured goods and to do that at a profit.

In February 1935, he spoke in the debate supporting the India Bill, which was to give self-government to India. Churchill voted against it but Sam spoke of India's legitimate aspirations, saying that she was a valuable customer to Lancashire, buying at one time 3,000 million yards of cotton cloth in one year. 'There is nothing intrinsic in the Bill,' he said, 'against Lancashire. But if the new legislature becomes anti-British, trade will not prosper.' He then reminded the House that it had learned from the Lancashire delegation which had been to India 18 months previously (the one he was on) that 'politically-minded India is extremely suspicious of Lancashire'. Then, after speaking of the duties and excise put on in Britain against imported cotton goods, he added: 'One of the results of our trade mission was to assuage that feeling of suspicion. We have now induced the Lancashire cotton manufacturers to use greater quantities of Indian cotton. It was, therefore, with great disappointment that the people of Lancashire learned that the recently concluded Indo-British Trade Agreement failed to find approval in the [Indian] Legislative Assembly. 'Lancashire,' he concluded, 'wants good-will and co-operation; and this view is shared by her political representatives – as will be seen when the division is taken.'

XI

Lifestyle

Sam, like his father, was an optimist. Other qualities for which Lord Coleraine said in his obituary he would be remembered were: 'his bluntness, his shrewdness, his utter lack of pomposity and his gaiety'. He enjoyed being a Member of Parliament and, although he was giving up Stockport, he did not intend to leave politics for good. However, although he received a letter from Lord Derby to say how glad he was to hear that he was seeking re-election, he did not get the Exchange Division of Manchester, for which he applied, and an important reason for his parliamentary career being a 'relatively minor one' (as Coleraine wrote) was that it was interrupted and he did not get back into parliament until 1938.

One of his last duties as the member for Stockport was, as chairman of the Lancashire members, to entertain Lord Derby in the House of Commons. He then voted against the India–Burma pact (which Lord Derby also opposed) and tabled several amendments to the Cotton Spinning Industry Bill, which he was disappointed, having failed to secure another seat, not to be able to defend when the House reassembled. In October he wrote an article in the *Evening Chronicle*: 'India: Our Best Ally'.

When he finally left Stockport, Fred and Helen Dehn arranged for the Heaton Moor Women's Conservative Association to present him and Kit with a large silver salver 'as a token of esteem and admiration'. Dehns was a firm of Manchester merchants exporting cotton cloth, largely to Africa, founded by a German-Jewish family. (In the First World War Fritz Dehn changed his name to Fred.)' James Agate, who was his elder son Paul's godfather, wrote in his autobiography: 'Dehns in Manchester was my second home.' When Paul grew up he made a name for himself as a poet, film critic and writer of film scripts. Olive, his sister, married the actor David Markham and their daughter Kika (named after her uncle Eric) also became an actress and married Corin Redgrave. The Dehns were the first resident guests that Sam and Kit had at Stroods, their new house in the country; they and their children spent Christmas there in 1932.

Other guests at Stroods were Sir Robert and Lady Gower. When they came for dinner with their daughter Pauline, she delighted the Hammersley girls by coming up to see them in bed and producing a screwdriver from the long skirts of her evening dress. Pauline was later CO of the Air Transport Auxiliary, which ferried planes for the RAF during the Second World War and in which Jadwiga Pilsudska, younger daughter of the late President of Poland, also served. Norman Crump, the economist, and his mathematician wife Patricia stayed at Stroods, giving their address (Leafland, Wood Vale, N.10) as 'Eights of 'Ighgate'. For Christmas 1936 Norman sent Sam a copy of his new book, co-written with George Clare, *The ABC of the Foreign Exchanges*. Lena and Frank Newnes were also regular visitors, as were the Lowises and the Laws, as well as old friends from before Sam and Kit were married, like Basil Groves and Ethel and Walter Wilson, who stayed with their three sons.

Sam's sister Gladys and her daughter Joanna, stayed; so did Sam's young Schofield cousin Terence Russell, who was working at Scotland Yard. From Kit's side of the family, her favourite Burbrook aunt, Mary (Ja), came for a week and her brother Jeff and his wife Eve also stayed. In 1934 Jeff and Eve announced that they had adopted a 14-year-old girl whose name, they said, was Susan Lee. But they did not bring her to stay until 1936 when, seeing how much like Jeff she looked, it became clear that she was their own daughter, born before they were married. Sue told her cousins that she had been in a home-school from which Eve and Jeff used to take her in the summer holidays; which explained why Peter, who knew nothing about her, had spent so many summers at Littlestone. Sam made a pun on Sue Lee, saying that she was not so much the wrong side of the blanket as under the bed (*sous lit*).

Sam liked making puns, and his teenage daughters were an appreciative audience. They also encouraged him when he made up facetious rhymes and laughed at his use of textile words, like fustian, dimity, cambric and bombazine, which he trotted out to amuse them. His sense of humour was recognised by many and mentioned in letters of sympathy on his death. But Kit did not always find him so funny, although she appreciated the little poems he wrote, often for the girls to recite on her birthdays. When she got fussed about staff shortages and things of that nature (and cooks did walk out), Sam knew better than to make a joke of it. He set about engaging others, telling her not to worry, all he wanted was for her to look beautiful for him.

His idealisation of her, however, did not make the relationship easy for her. She was shrewd enough to know, whatever he said to the contrary, that she was not exceptional and, as she got older, her lack of self-confidence increased. She always felt that she had let him down in not giving him a son and, as he loved babies, each time she was pregnant (several times miscarrying) she hoped that it would be a boy. Sam, however, liked being surrounded by women and felt comfortable with them, which made him popular with the women on his constituency committees. But after the Lavender affair, he was careful not to let another woman get too close to him; partly because of Kit's watchful jealousy and partly because, accepting her version that he had been trapped by Lavender, he did not trust himself.

However, he still went dancing, considering it to be a

pleasurable exercise. He taught his daughters to dance, often clutching a pillow as he demonstrated, and then, as he took one as a partner, the other one or two would take cushions and dance round beside him. When he danced with Kit they looked like an exhibition pair. He was always careful about his appearance and liked to wear the latest and most fashionable clothes. He had more than one suit of tails and a drawerful of stiff-fronted shirts with detachable collars to wear with white bow ties. He was fussy about his hair, especially now it was receding, and had it cut and dressed in a special way, following his hairdresser, Viccari, when he moved from one establishment to another. He went to Anderson & Sheppard in Savile Row for his suits and was punctilious about the cuffs of his shirts, with cuff-links, showing an exact amount below his jacket. His long narrow feet were only comfortable in hand-made shoes. But it was not only in fashion that he liked to keep up to date; above all, he wanted his businesses to be in the forefront of industry with all the newest machinery.

In London he had a flat where he worked with his secretary who came in daily; first in Marsham Street and later in Robert Street, Adelphi, moving to Tufton Court in 1935 and a year later to 50 Sloane Street. In spite of no longer being able to speak in parliament, he continued to take an interest in public finance and in November 1935 wrote an article in *The Banker*, which again urged a more expansionist monetary policy. At S. Noton Ltd he appointed A.C. Tugwell as Secretary, a job that he kept until after Sam's death in 1965. In his letter of sympathy Tugwell wrote of Sam: 'I shall always recall with gratitude his outstanding leadership at Notons and the guidance he so readily gave to me personally for over thirty years.'

Sam spent one week in London and the next in Manchester, where he stayed at the Clarendon Club in Mosley Street from 1934, when he joined it, until it closed in the 1960s. He enjoyed being able to entertain his friends and business associates and, no doubt, when in Manchester, embellished a bit on his exploits in London and the south. His stockbroker, Anthony Sancroft-Baker, lived and worked there, so did his accountant, Percy Westhead. Percy Westhead was a close friend and many of the letters that passed between them, as Sam sent in his accounts and tax returns, mention topics of the day on which Sam sought his friend's advice.

From his Manchester base Sam attended meetings at his cotton mills in Oldham, Shaw, Middleton and Royton as well as at S. Noton Ltd's Oldham factory. He was also at this time still paying off his father's debts and winding up his father's affairs. This involved him in some hard bargaining with, among others, William Noton, who was a substantial creditor in the Delta and Rugby mills. Among Sam's papers is a note in his own hand: 'after considering liabilities, Father's estate was left with a deficit of £35,000.' It was a matter of some satisfaction to him that he was able to reorganise and amalgamate many of his late father's mills so as to set up trusts for each of his sisters and that between 1936 and 1938 he was able to get permission for shares in the Devon, Soudan and Fernhurst mills to be quoted not only on the Manchester Exchange but also on the London Stock Exchange.

He took on another directorship in 1936, in Mandlebergs, a firm of rainwear manufacturers in Pendleton (incorporated 1889) that was reorganising. The rubber-proofing plant was modernised after a visit by two of their engineers to the USA, for which there are notes in Sam's own hand. Valstar, their trade name, was owed money from Italy but could not be credited with it on account of the sanctions imposed during the Abyssinian war. However, by 1937 Mandlebergs were making an annual profit of some £40,000. The Mandlebergs had been interested in viscose rayon yarn since its early days and later, when they took over Harbens in Golborne, Sam joined them on that board as well.

By the end of 1935 he was trying to buy the freehold of Stroods but Lord Rankeillour did not want to sell, so instead he bought Saxon Court, Buxted. This house had been built for the Grieves of Oldham and, before Sam extended the ground floor and added a room tall enough to take his huge Victorian bookcase, looked not unlike his old home, Stoneleigh Hall. There was a short drive, with a pair of cottages at the gates, stables and a paddock for the children's pony, greenhouses and a walled kitchen garden. (Stoneleigh Hall was destroyed after the Second World War but the stable block was for a time used as a lending library before becoming a pavilion for the public park.)

As Saxon Court (soon abbreviated to Saxons) was a freehold, Kit felt justified in spending money on it. Here was a chance for her to put her interior-decorating ideas into practice and she very much enjoyed getting the exact colours she wanted, like a very pale green-blue that involved filling the bath with water to demonstrate to the painters. They remonstrated with her when she wanted the ceilings in all the reception rooms, as well as the walls, painted in high gloss, but she got her way because she wanted the house to be as light and full of sunshine as possible. She had wall-to-wall carpets in the bedrooms but downstairs there were only antique carpets on the light oak floors that she had scraped and limed. She also had the staircase in limed oak, for which the bannisters were made by repeating 'S'es and sugar sticks (almost Sam's initials). Both she and Sam smoked, liking a cigarette after meals, but neither of them was a serious smoker and Sam had given it up long before he died. As Saxons had extensive greenhouses, he started his collection of orchids and began to take an interest in gardening.

The last time he played golf seriously was at Crowborough in 1931 for the parliamentary team against the locals. One of the members of the Crowborough club was Roger Eckersley, who worked for the BBC and in World War II was head of their American service. When Sam went to India he asked Roger to keep an eye on Kit while he was away. Roger's son Timothy later married Penelope.

The Eckersleys were not, however, his closest neighbours. These were the Maufes who lived at Shepherds Hill, just across the valley from Saxons. Edward Maufe was an architect, later responsible for Guildford Cathedral but at this time designing St Andrew's Presbyterian church in Pont Street. His wife Prudence (who dressed like a Quaker) was manageress at Heals. Their son, Gareth, caught a mysterious virus and died before either of his parents. Prudence wrote to Kit to say that the doctors held out no hope for him. 'His brain is good. He goes to the office for a few hours a day, can walk, or rather shuffle, about 50 yards, has to haul his two legs into a car and that is all', she wrote.' 'No pain, thank God. But it is utterly heartbreaking. We only have ONE son.'

In the Saxons visitors' book names of old friends were repeated, but now there were also increasing numbers of the children's school friends. Sam encouraged them to discuss the affairs of the moment with him, often by deliberately taking an opposite point of view. Far from showing disapproval of his own two eldest daughters' leaning towards socialism, he gave them a year's subscription to the Left Book Club and obtained permission for them to have the books delivered monthly to their boarding school. Some of the school friends' parents also stayed, such as the artist couples Jocelyn and Elaine Bodley and Cuthbert Orde (called Turps) and his wife, Lady Eileen (Wellesley), who was paralysed and painted with the brush in her mouth, sitting in a wheelchair. Turps was attracted to Kit but, although he crooned her the song 'The night is young, the breezes sing of it. Can't you get into the swing of it?', she would not respond.

Other weekend guests were Simon Harcourt-Smith and his wife Rosamund, who, although over 40, was expecting her first child. Simon was writing his book *The Last of Uptake* and set up his typewriter on a card table on the lawn. Mabel Parr, who was in Europe with her grown-up daughter, Clarisse, stayed. She had a house in the South

80

of France where Kit and Sam and the girls went on a visit in 1936, just after the last of the Hammersley daughters, Philippa Juliet, was born. In early 1937 Kit and Sam and their two eldest daughters went to France again, this time with Dick and Mary Law, staying in a chateau on the Loire. The Abdication crisis broke on their return.

King Edward VIII's tour of the South Wales coalfields, where there was mass unemployment, had been a success, increasing his popularity. Here, people thought, was a monarch who cared for the common man and, what is more, had openly declared that he would do something to improve his lot. This put Baldwin in a difficult position: kings should not interfere in politics. Besides, in standing with the Archbishop of Canterbury against the idea of a divorcee (and an American) becoming queen, he was supported by the bulk of British, conformist, middle-class opinion. Either Edward had to give up Mrs Simpson or he had to give up the throne.

In the Hammersley household the unfolding drama was most closely followed. Nanny's sister was the personal maid to Sir Walter Monckton's wife (and had been since the latter was 11 years old). Her family, the Colyer-Fergussons, lived at Ightham Mote, where the Hammersley children, when they were younger, had often been taken by Nanny so that she could have Sunday lunch with her sister. Monckton was legal adviser to the King and mediator between him and Baldwin. *Time* magazine wrote all about the King and Mrs Simpson, and Kit and the girls were reading it avidly, long before anything appeared in the British press. They believed firmly in the power of love and were on the side of the King and romance. Sam, however, had doubts about Edward's character and the wisdom of his association with the Nazis. The Saar had been returned to Germany in 1935 and in 1936 the Germans marched back into the Ruhr unopposed. The British Embassy in Berlin was sending warning reports to London but they were either unread or disbelieved.

XII

Member of Parliament for East Willesden

In 1937 Sam's sister Gladys took a flat in Vienna so that she could be with her daughter Joanna, who was there having her voice trained. Penelope also went to Vienna and stayed as a paying guest with the Esterhazys to learn German. When Gladys developed a serious liver complaint, Sam went to visit her and to discuss her treatment with the doctors. By Christmas she was sufficiently recovered to travel and she, Joanna and Penelope all returned to England. With them they brought back first-hand information about the political divisions in Austria, which had its own Nazi party, and the fears of liberals and intellectuals for their freedom; fears that were fully realised when, in March 1938, Hitler's troops marched into Austria, declaring it a single state with Germany.

Europe was polarising between Communism and Fascism. Sam's secretary, Barbara, who had left to go and fight for the Republicans in Spain, arrived to find them already defeated. Jewish refugees were arriving in England from all over Europe, fleeing Nazi persecution. As the likelihood of war increased, some British businesses with international connections found themselves in difficulties. One of these was Forsyth & Partners, where Richard Law was a director with Edward Forsyth, Sylvester Gates and Albert Kohan. Sam, at Law's request, went in as Managing Director. The assets included the Belgian-based Amalgamated Petroleum Trust; a Swiss firm, Afina; Tecalemit; the Podrinje antimony mines in

Yugoslavia run by Albert Kohan's brother-in-law; and oil wharves on Canvey Island in the Thames. From this time on the Forsyths and the Kohan connections were frequent visitors at Saxon Court.

Eddy Forsyth was a Scotsman who spoke good German. He had a fine tenor voice, which he exercised in the bath, singing German lieder. Both he and his German wife Marta were pilots and had their private plane, in which they attended the sporting rallies that were held throughout Europe in the 1930s. He was more of a playboy than a businessman and she had ambitions to be a model. Their house, 30 Great Cumberland Place, was bigger than 44 Princes Gardens and had cavernous basement kitchens, but only the two of them lived in it until their daughter was born in 1939, soon after which their marriage broke up.

Albert Kohan was a Russian Jew, born near Kiev, the son of a rich sugar-planter who sent him to study in Belgium. During the First World War he became a Belgian citizen and joined the Belgian Intelligence Service. He met his wife, Nadia Liebowitz, as she was returning with her two small sons from a holiday in Baden Baden, and persuaded her to elope with him. They got married in Berlin and stayed there a year while their daughter Marion was born, then, as Nadia did not like Belgium, they settled in Paris. However, Albert was a great womaniser and, although he adored his daughter, did not stay living with his wife for very long. Business obliged him to travel a lot and he had many mistresses. In England he lived with Natasha Cruthers (another Russian), for whom he rented a flat in Basil Street. When Penelope, who was studying journalism at King's College, London, stayed a couple of nights with her, she reported that the full red lips that were such a feature of Natasha's appearance were not there in the mornings. Both Natasha and Albert's daughter Marion often stayed at Saxon Court, and after their visits Albert would send Kit baskets of wild strawberries and Belgian chocolates by Air France, with which he travelled frequently and where he was well known as one of their first regular passengers.

Sylvester Gates was a barrister by profession and was to become Chairman of Tecalemit Ltd and later Deputy Chairman of Westminster Bank. In June 1936 he, with Albert Kohan and three other directors, set up the Canvey Island storage facilities of Forsyth & Partners as London & Coastal Oil Wharfs; a company of which Sam also later became a director. Sylvester's wife Pauline was the daughter of Algernon Newton, the artist, and sister of the actor Robert Newton.

Another colourful character who came into Sam's life at this time was Harvey Brabazon Combe. Harvey lived at Sedlescombe and his daughter went to school with the Hammersley girls. He and Sam were such good friends that Kit called him Sam's buddy. Harvey, like Sam, was at home in a man's club; and indeed it was often in one of Sam's London clubs that they met. Sam relaxed with Harvey, who liked a drink and a cigar and did not criticise, and he admired his enterprise. Sometimes he had a lot of money and sometimes he had to borrow because he was broke. His wife Alice (called Terry), who looked like a duchess but had been a chorus girl, sometimes behaved as though she were the former and sometimes the latter. She referred to their butler as 'that bloody boy Alfred' even in his presence, but if the girls did anything so vulgar as attempt to blow their noses at the dinner table, they were sent out of the room. Harvey smiled indulgently whatever she did and, taking Sam off, left the women to play bezique.

In August 1935 Harvey brought a certain Treviranus to see Sam. The Hammersley girls and Harvey's daughter Eileen, in spite of seeing some Czechoslovakian shoes which they were told he had come to ask their fathers to promote, believed that he wore a bulletproof waistcoat and was a spy. (Sam still held shares in British Czech Shoes as late as 1963!) Treviranus had in fact come to ask Harvey to help him release several consignments of Bata shoes that

84

had been impounded at Tilbury. To do this he had to pay off his outstanding debts to British banks. Harvey did not have the money to do this himself and introduced him to Sam. In exchange, Treviranus was offering Harvey and Sam an interest in his 'experimental portable 160-mm talkie camera' if they would set up a company to promote it and apply for the British patent. The original camera proposal, signed by Treviranus, was witnessed by Fred Dehn. Treviranus was not the first or the last to come to Sam for finance for an 'invention' so Kit was not surprised when she heard nothing more of the camera company. Harvey was soon to become an agent for Bofors guns and, when war was declared, was commissioned to buy guns for the British Government.

In July 1938, there was a by-election in the constituency of East Willesden and Sam stood in place of the retiring Conservative. In his election campaign he advertised himself as 'a businessman' and had posters printed which showed him wearing a dark jacket, striped trousers and a homburg hat, standing up in a boat 'Steering for Peace' between the two rocks of Unemployment and War. His election address pledged him to social reforms: support for holidays with pay and a national service of midwives. He was opposed by Maurice Orbach, who, although he was a member of the Communist Party, stood for Labour.

East Willesden was described at the time as a London dormitory constituency with a shifting population and a high proportion of Jews. But although the numbers on the electoral register had increased since the First World War, the percentage of those voting had gone down. Many were indifferent, others had moved away and, because the election took place in late July, others were on holiday.

However, Sam held the seat for the Conservatives although Maurice, who was Jew, had been a local councillor until disqualified from holding office by the National Executive of the Labour Party, and had contested the seat at the previous general election. The Communist v Fascist confrontation was very strong at this time and slogans were chalked up on the walls by both factions. Sam, in one of his election speeches, made a point of saying that he was against dictatorships, whether of the Left or the Right. The *Zionist Review* reported him, during the campaign, as being in favour of a national home for the Jews in Palestine and later he was to take a prominent part in the Anglo–Israel Association. Yet Maurice Orbach refused to shake hands with him after the poll, he and his supporters shouting: '*Heil*, von Hammersley!', and Sam had to be protected by the police in order to get out of the hall.

Soon after parliament reassembled in September, Chamberlain returned from his meeting with Hitler in Munich, at which he agreed to the Czechoslovakian settlement for 'peace in our time'. This was debated in parliament over several days and Richard Law made a significant speech. 'Czechoslovakia,' said Chamberlain, which he had agreed with Hitler should be divided between Germany and Hungary, 'was the natural ally of Germany, not of France'. Few thinking people, however, felt that this removed the threat of war.

In February 1939 Sam spoke 'as a member of the commercial community' in the debate on currency and banknotes. He also continued to speak in all the debates on the cotton industry. The President of the Board of Trade said at this time that, of the two members then in the House who knew most about cotton, one was Hammersley. During the first half of 1939 he sat on a committee of the House of Commons to consider an Enabling Bill for the cotton trade and spoke on the Cotton Industry Reorganisation Bill. He also wrote letters to the *Manchester Guardian* on the subject and addressed the Edinburgh House Club in his constituency on 'The Cotton Industry & Britain's Economic Strength'.

Throughout 1939 opposition to Chamberlain's leadership had been hardening among Conservative backbenchers. There were three groups, each with its own proposed alternative leader, all feeling that, although his government was called a national government, it was not sufficiently broad-based. An indication of the way in which Sam was thinking came when, in July, he said in the House that, although he did not want to embarrass the government, he wished to urge it to make use of Winston Churchill's services. Yet Chamberlain, in spite of announcing an end to his policy of appeasement, spoke and acted as though he believed there was a limit to Hitler's territorial ambitions and that it would be possible to come to terms with him.

Life went on as before. In May Sam invited a party of 45 children from deprived parts of Willesden to spend the day at Saxons; in June he went over to Guernsey, without Kit who would not go with him, in response to reports that her properties there were in need of repair; and in July Penelope was presented at court.

Yet underneath this apparent normality there was a growing feeling of unease. Sam made a speech in his constituency with the title 'Will There Be War?' He also declared himself in favour of conscription. He knew first-hand from Harvey Combe of the shortage of guns and there was an air force demonstration to Westminster to protest at the serious shortage of planes. In July he attended a meeting of the Anglo-French Parliamentary Committee for a discussion on '*Les Evénements d'Extreme Urgence Vues de France*'.

He decided, however, to go ahead with a holiday in the South of France with Kit and three of his daughters, where they stayed in the same hotel in St Tropez as the astronomer Sir James Jeans and his German wife. But they had to return in a hurry towards the end of August as, with the worsening international situation, a three-line whip went out and parliament was recalled.

XIII

World War II

On 1st September Germany invaded Poland and on the 3rd, because Hitler did not withdraw, the British declared war on Germany. This was the first time parliament had met on a Sunday for a hundred years. Afterwards Sam went to the library of the House of Commons and, overcome by the emotion of the occasion, wrote a striking article for the *Willesden Chronicle* entitled 'The Way to Peace'.

Air-raid sirens sounded in London immediately after Chamberlain's broadcast message and many people, fearing that there would not only be bombing but even gas attacks, fled to the country. But as nothing happened, after a few weeks many of them returned and, apart from making blackout curtains, filling sandbags and other air-raid precaution exercises, life continued much as before. British soldiers joined the French in the Maginot Line and, believing the Germans to be doing as little as they were, sang: *We'll Hang Out Our Washing on the Siegfried Line* and *Run, Rabbit, Run*. At Saxon Court there was still a joint of beef for Sunday lunch and McKenzie, Sam and the girls sang: 'Carve me off a slice or two, I'll tell you when to stop; all I want is a little bit off the top'. But Germany, having conquered Poland, was building up her forces so as to go round the Maginot Line and attack France through the Low Countries and, in order not to be stabbed in the back by the Soviet Union, signed a friendship pact with Stalin, allowing him to invade eastern Poland.

At home there were plans for the dispersal of non-essential members of the population from the big cities, and one Sunday morning a contingent of children evacuated from London arrived in East Sussex unexpectedly. Countess Castle Stewart (née Guggenheim), who was chairwoman of the local Women's Institute, was the only person available to meet them. 'It's a good job somebody is not in church,' she said to Kit, persuading her to take eleven of them at Saxon Court, escorted by one mother.

On their first night, although several rooms and separate beds were provided for them, they all went to the same room, four or five in the one big bed and the rest underneath it. After several weeks, other homes were found for most of them in the district or, like Mrs Morris and her three children, they got homesick for London and went back. Leslie Hardesty, however, stayed for four years and Jenniver, who was a year his senior, taught him to ride and groom horses and make hay. As he had impetigo when he arrived, for which yeast was prescribed, all the Hammersley girls were obliged to eat raw baker's yeast with him, to set a good example. His little brother Denis, aged four, joined him a year later but stayed for a shorter time. Denis could not understand why Nanny did no cooking and, when he was not hiding from 'li'le ol 'Itler' under the nursery table, he was tugging at her skirt asking when she was going to get the dinner.

As a reservist, Sam was recalled for military service and was immediately made responsible for estimating the costs of the kitting-up, provisioning and general preparation of a unit, for which his financial calculations proved, much to his satisfaction, to be totally accurate. He got himself a smart new uniform with a Tank Corps beret and was photographed against a background of sandbags outside the Constitutional Club in Walm Lane, Willesden. He and Kit each made a speech and then were photographed together, Kit looking slim and stiff, in a hard little hat with a veil. Sam was happy to be Captain Hammersley again; it made him feel young, and in the House, like all serving officers, he was referred to as 'the Honourable and Gallant Gentleman'.

Speaking on 21 September, he asked the Chancellor of the Exchequer whether he would take steps to ascertain the value of capital owned by those liable to income tax, but was told to wait for the Emergency Budget. When this was debated a week later, he spoke again. The heavy burdens imposed by the Budget had to be shouldered, he said, but it was important not to finance this war as the last by leaving a crippling debt to future generations. Looking ahead, he said he felt steps should be taken to prevent rentiers getting fat while industry suffered. He welcomed the proposed increase in income tax, death duties and super tax but felt that richer people should also make a contribution from capital and wanted all taxpayers to make a 'return of capital' so that, at the end of the war they could be taxed on its increase (if any). The Chancellor of the Exchequer answered that he was 'studying the point' but Sam urged him to 'do it now'.

In October the Cotton Industry Reorganisation (postponement) Bill was read for the second time and Sam spoke in favour of price-fixing; not this time the fixing of minimum prices, as was originally proposed when the cotton industry was working under capacity, but maximum prices to prevent war profiteering. In a subsequent speech the President of the Board of Trade, Oliver Stanley, supported him in this. He was not, however, agreeable to setting up a Cotton Board (as Sam wanted) but proposed instead a Cotton Controller, with new powers.

Later in the year Sam spoke again, in the debate on the Finance Bill, re excess profits tax, saying that the basis on which it was proposed that this should be levied was particularly adverse to the cotton trade since the base years chosen had, for them, all been disastrous ones. Thus, he said, the Excess Profits Bill, while designed to prevent profiteering, was going to deprive previously depressed trades of a reasonable profit. He also spoke, in committee, on the Prices of Goods Bill, giving instances of

90

large retail profits on cotton goods and asking the President of the Board of Trade to fix margins. An amendment he proposed to the Cotton & Rayon Bill was accepted. He also spoke in the Supply Committee debate, urging curtailment of civilian purchasing power. The notes for this speech indicate that he was thinking about preserving earning power for the future.

His diaries show that during 1939 he attended 30 parliamentary debates, asked some 40 questions and had 29 constituency engagements. He also attended monthly dinners in the House with the Economic Committee. He went to nine balls or dances (some of these were constituency functions such as the Junior Empire League Ball in Willesden), was at Goodwood for the races and went shooting some 12 times. On 15 December he was invited to a shoot at Birch Grove with six other neighbours of Harold Macmillan's, most of them MPs, among them Admiral Beamish, MP for Lewes. Beamish lost his elder son in the war but the younger one, Tufton (later Lord Chelwood), succeeded him in Lewes and his book *Must Night Fall?*, published in 1950, exposed the true situation in Communist-dominated Eastern Europe at a time when the West was still starry-eyed about Russia.

By the end of 1939 Sam had given up the small flat he had in Sloane Street and taken a larger one at 19 Chesham Street, where he was looked after by a living-in housekeeper, Margaret Allen. His next-door neighbour was Lady Harcourt, at whose musical evenings he met her daughters Griselda and Diana (née Gould) and their two suitors, Yehudi Menuhin and Louis Kentner. Kit was now rarely able to go to London as she was busy at Saxon Court looking after the house and the children, growing vegetables and rearing chickens. She still had Nanny and McKenzie but otherwise had to rely on the help of local girls after her last two resident maids had been repatriated, one an Austrian cook who left tearfully and the other a German Nazi.

Sam was now rising 47 and had put on weight, and by

November, when he had to go for a medical, was pronounced unfit for active service and discharged from the army. Soon afterwards he joined the Home Guard and his future son-in-law, Timothy Eckersley, photographed him roaring with laughter, about to go out on patrol, his smart new uniform hidden beneath the accoutrement of tin hat, gas mask, thermos flask and rug, armed only with his own sporting gun.

It was not only the Home Guard that was short of weapons and on 13 December, during a debate in secret session, Sam spoke of the growing concern that he and many others felt about the pace of British rearmament. 'Our tanks,' he said on this occasion, 'are woefully inadequate in numbers and unsatisfactory in performance.' He also said that the supply of Bofors guns, made in Britain by Nuffield, was unsatisfactory both in quality and numbers 'owing to over-optimistic quoting'.

Leo Amery, who as early as October 1938 in the debate on the Munich Agreement had urged Neville Chamberlain to organise for war, also spoke in this debate, and a group of like-minded Conservative backbenchers, which including Sam, were rallying behind him. On this occasion Amery had said that the government's happy-go-lucky attitude would put the country at grave peril if it were called upon to face the well-organised dictatorships. Now that the war had come, it was imperative that those perils be faced up to. In March 1940 he initiated a debate on the resolution that Chamberlain should resign, but this only resulted in the formation of a War Cabinet, while retaining Chamberlain as leader.

However, the talk throughout the Conservative Party for the need of a new leader was growing and, although Lord Halifax was a runner-up to Churchill as favourite, he had the big disadvantage of being a member of the House of Lords. There was much coming and going between Birch Grove, where Macmillan and Amery conferred together, and Dolloways, the house immediately opposite Saxon Court where Law now lived. For many months Sam was closely involved in these events, taking an active part in the consultations. He was particularly anxious about both the supply and design of tanks, and in April, when conscription was introduced, asked for a secret session of the House to discuss the 'grave deficiencies of the fighting services'. It was his question to the House of Commons on 7 May, voicing grave dissatisfaction in the conduct of the war, that acted as a 'warming up' and 'introduction' for the big debate that followed.

Churchill, as First Lord of the Admiralty, had advocated sending the navy to Norway (as in 1916 he had sent it to the Dardanelles) and, after the results turned out to be equally disastrous, a debate was called for in the House. A three-line whip went out and MPs were warned that 'a division of the utmost importance may take place', so that by ten o'clock on the evening of 10 May the House was packed. Kit sat in the gallery with Lady Dorothy Macmillan and Mary Law, watching as the excitement mounted. As Chamberlain came under fire, both from the Labour Party and the Conservative backbenches, Churchill tried to take some responsibility upon himself, defending his chief. But Amery's speech, ending with: 'In the name of God, go!' showed the strength of feeling.

By the next morning there was a Vote of Censure on the table, put down by the Labour Party, and the debate went into its second day. Lloyd George spoke of the 'good of the country', and Duff Cooper, knowing that Churchill would defend Chamberlain and wind up for the government, warned the House against his persuasive oratory, saying that this was a matter above party politics. Sam was among the 33 Conservatives who voted against the government. Order papers were waved, members shouted 'Resign!' and some even started singing *Rule, Britannia*.

By the following morning, as news came through that Belgium and Holland had been invaded, Churchill was confirmed as Prime Minister and the Labour leader, Clement Atlee, his deputy. At last the 'phoney war' was

93

over and there was a national government not only in name but in spirit.

Churchill flew over to France three times to encourage French resistance, but they had no reserves and the plan to cut through the German pincer failed. France became divided and their fleet took refuge in Oran. But when an appeal was made to Admiral Darlan to bring it out and join the Free French, he failed to respond to the call and it was sunk by the British to prevent it falling into German hands. Individual Frenchmen, however, responded to General De Gaulle's call to join him in London, and all members of the Polish forces that had been stationed in France tried to get to Britain. Signposts were removed from road junctions, blackout restrictions were enforced, food rationing began and everyone was issued with identity cards. Clothing coupons were issued the following year.

Kit received a letter from *Horizon* magazine (edited by Cyril Connolly) which was signed by Peter Watson, Stephen Spender, Henry Moore and Herbert Read. It was dated 15 May 1940 and in it they appealed for help for Dylan Thomas:

> He has been called up at a moment when he is very much in debt and unless he is able to raise £70 almost immediately his wife will be turned out of their house and their few possessions seized. We think you will agree with us that something should be done to prevent this happening to one of the most remarkable young English Poets at a moment when he is serving his country.

On 4 June Churchill made his famous speech, in secret session: 'We will fight them on the beaches ... We will never surrender', extracts from which were later broadcast to the nation.

XIV

Wartime

Immediately after the fall of France, Mary Law went to America, where she left her two little boys, Martin and Andrew, and returned to England. Lallie Lee Lowis also went, staying with her four children and their English nanny (Geoffrey was in the navy). Sam suggested that Kit might go with Nanny and the two youngest girls. But Kit did not like the idea of leaving Sam on his own, nor was she confident that she could manage by herself. She kept a letter from Nanny, who did not want to go either. 'You must do as you think best', Nanny wrote, 'but I am not any more a young woman. Jenniver doesn't want to go.' Jenniver had a companion in Sarah Macmillan, who stayed at Saxons as Birch Grove was given over to a children's home. Both girls were mad about horses, riding and grooming their ponies together, and in the evening they played piano duets.

Another reason why Kit decided not to go to America was that in July Penelope and Timothy Huxley Eckersley were going to get married. Penelope, who had received her Journalist Diploma from King's College, London, just before war was declared, was working as Assistant Almoner at the Kent & Sussex Hospital in Tunbridge Wells. Ever since Dunkirk, the Kent & Sussex Hospital had been full of wounded soldiers, many of them French, and following the occupation of Holland, Belgium, Denmark and Norway, men of fighting age from all these countries began making their way to Britain to continue the fight against Hitler, rallying to their governments-in-exile.

When Richard Law, who was Under-Secretary at the Foreign Office, had to invite the King of Norway for a weekend at Dolloways, he was at a loss as to how to entertain him. The Hammersley girls suggested that David Stutchbury, who was a good pianist, should be asked to play for him. David, who was a pilot in Aerial Reconnaissance, often came over to Saxons to play the piano and to play tennis. His widowed mother, Rosamund, was staying at the Maufes' at Shepherds Hill with her four children. She had played the violin at Glyndebourne in its early days when they only had an amateur orchestra there, and the whole family was musical. The Laws did not have a piano so the 'concert' took place at Saxons. David Stutchbury ended up not only playing the piano for the King of Norway but also playing tennis at Saxons with him and the Crown Prince, and the entries 'Haakon R' and 'Olav, C.P.o N.' appeared in the Saxon Court visitors' book.

When in August 1940 Germany started aerial attacks on London and the south-east, it was generally supposed that the invasion was about to begin. In country pubs people told tales of the resistance they would put up with guile, pitchforks and fierce dogs. Pillboxes were built at road junctions and ditches dug along the coast. Sam, who was Joint Secretary of the Parliamentary Palestine Committee, appealed for the formation of a Jewish battalion, knowing that 50,000 were ready and willing to serve. Even when, in late September, Hitler gave up his daytime attacks and switched to the night bombing of London, invasion was still expected.

On 10 May 1941 the chamber of the House of Commons was destroyed by incendiary bombs, together with the voting lobbies, but firefighters isolated the fire so that nothing further was affected. Before the clearing-up started, Sam went with two of his daughters to view the devastation and the girls came away with a piece of wrought-iron from the old 'bar' of the House. Until the middle of June, when the Lords invited the Commons to

96

occupy their chamber, the Commons met at Church House. (The new Commons chamber was not ready until late 1950.)

Although there were plenty of fighting men in Britain of many nationalities, every kind of weaponry with which to arm them was in short supply. The Polish planes that had been flown to Romania had been interned and not many Polish ships had escaped from the Baltic. Few French ships or planes joined De Gaulle, and the British fleet was fully stretched. After the Battle of Britain, in which two Polish squadrons took part, the number of fighting planes was dangerously low. The only supplies not coming from British factories were from Roosevelt's agreement to sell unwanted war materials and laid-up ships from America. It is not surprising, therefore, that when in June 1941 Germany invaded the Soviet Union, Churchill welcomed Stalin as an ally. The Soviet Union, however, gave no material aid to Britain; on the contrary, British sailors suffered terrible losses and great hardship on the Arctic convoys ferrying goods to Russia. The only advantage was that German troops were henceforth fighting on two fronts.

It was not long before Sam got complaints from his constituency that schools were being used by the Communist Party and that Communist Party loudspeaker vans were touring Willesden. Natasha Cruthers said: 'under Hitler some people can be happy but nobody can be happy under Stalin.' She urged Kit to 'get Sam to give you jewels not jewellery' and, pawning her huge cabochon emerald ring with him, she fled to America.

Eddy Forsyth, with his flying skills and excellent German, had been offered a commission in RAF Intelligence. However, when he boasted indiscreetly about it in his club, the commission was withdrawn. Marta, who was also a pilot, could not joint the Air Transport Auxiliary because she was German by birth. (Her mother was interned in the Isle of Man.)

Sam built a wooden frame in the hedge in front of

97

Saxons on which to rest his Winchester gun with its telescope sight, and when the invasion scare retreated, the frame, which overlooked the rabbit warren, was used in conjunction with the shotgun to supplement the family meat ration. Kit bought a small churn to make milk into butter which she took with her everywhere, turning the handle all the time as the butter took a long time to come. Britain was in a state of siege. Food convoys in the Atlantic were being attacked by U-boats. Any off-ration food was husbanded and jealously guarded. Mary Law boasted to Kit that she had found a wonderful field for mushrooms but she would not reveal where it was and, knowing that Kit liked breakfast in bed, said that anyway she would have to get up early. Kit, however, was intrigued and one day, going out before breakfast, found Mary in the Saxons fields!

In July Sam had to rush down from London in the middle of the week as he was anxious about his third daughter, Priscilla, who had fallen off her bicycle and been found unconscious at the roadside. She lay in a darkened room for several days and it was feared that she would lose the sight in one eye. In fact her sight was permanently impaired but she completed her art course in Brighton and went on to get a degree from the Architectural Association.

Although Sam had tried both in April 1940, and again in early May, to get Chamberlain to allow the House to go into secret session so that the inadequacies of the armed forces could be properly discussed, he had not been successful. But after Churchill came to power, on 20 June he got the opportunity to make the speech he had prepared.

The tanks that Britain had in France during 1939–40 were more heavily armoured than their German counterparts and supplied with 2-pounder guns that were more potent than Germany's 37-millimetre; however, Germany had ten heavy armoured divisions on the Western Front and Britain only one. More importantly, Germany had the swift, co-ordinated panzers which neither the French nor the British high command took seriously in spite of warning by France's Deuxième Bureau, which had known about them as early as 1935. Neither had they been convinced of their usefulness, even when they were so successful in the Polish campaign. As Sam said in his speech:

Of all the disappointments and discouragements which the British public have had to bear, no disillusionment has been more bitter than the realisation that our tanks are woefully inadequate in numbers and unsatisfactory in performance. Invented by British genius, the one great tactical surprise of the last war, tanks are playing an overwhelmingly important role in this war. It is natural to assume that what we have introduced we can develop, that with the great advances that have taken place in engines, metals, arms and armaments in the last twenty years, the substantial production which we enjoyed then would be completely overshadowed by the achievements of today. Unfortunately the facts contradict these reasonable anticipations. The German superiority in numbers is in the neighbourhood of 20 to 1, the French, over 10 to 1. In relation to the size of our own Army, the size of the Royal Armoured Corps is paltry; in relation to that of Germany it is well-nigh negligible.

I intervene in this debate to make some observations on the causes that have led to this parlous position and to offer some suggestions as to remedies. If there had not been a change of Government, I should have considered it my duty to endeavour to expose our shortcomings. In particular, I should have thought it necessary to attack the former Minister of Supply for his failure to take adequate and even reasonable steps to deal with the position; for his obstinate refusal to face the facts and his persistent efforts to deceive those, and they were many, who knew more about the position than he allowed himself to know. But, as the Prime Minister said, this is not the time for post-mortems, and neither is it a time to emphasize or advertise our deficiencies. I feel sure that it is in accordance with the temper of the House, as I know it is in accordance with the temper of the Nation, that I should confine myself to constructive analysis and constructive suggestions.

He could not do this, he said, without giving an idea of the lack of continuity in tank development under the Mechanisation Board, which had had three different directors in the last three years and was made up of individuals from different branches of the army, none of whom had experience of tanks. Normally the development of any technical and mechanical problem involves continuity. The experience of the past forms the basis for the improvements of the present, one man building on what his predecessors have consolidated. But, this had not been the case with the development of tanks by the British army with the result that the tanks now in use and in production, were not developments of tanks they were the physical embodiment of sporadic ideas; one tank after another designed to show *some* advance in a particular direction while perpetuating errors that were eliminated in other machines made many years ago. When war broke out, the only tanks either in production, or in design for production, were elaborate, costly vehicles, intended for service in the Empire, each with some 6,000 different parts and requiring some 50,000 different machine and assembly operations. Two factors; ease of production and the ability to negotiate difficult ground, both of which are now of overwhelming importance, were neglected.

After speaking again at some length about the Mechanisation Board, its constitution and inadequacies, he said that freeing it from the control of the army and incorporating it in the Ministry of Supply had done nothing to make it more efficient, neither had the appointment of a

Director-General of Tank Production been a success. Production figures were appallingly bad. 'What', he asked, 'shall we do now?'

First: speed up production. This speeding up of production involves two separate activities:– better organisation to harmonise the flow of parts to the works, and immediate critical examination of design and methods of production with a view to the elimination of unnecessary refinements, the introduction of commercial specifications and improvements in methods of construction.

Second: There is much unused ability in relation to tanks. By harnessing the great resources of improvisation latent in our engineering works, there is no doubt that within a few weeks we could turn out light tanks at the rate of scores, if not hundreds, per week (light tanks, which would be of the greatest use for Home defence purposes). There is nothing wonderful or frightening about the German tanks in this war. There has been, however, an element of surprise in the methods in which tanks have been used. The co-operation not only between tanks and other arms of the fighting services but also between heavy and light tanks and tanks plus wireless efficiency, where they have been able to stage a performance impossible with tanks alone.

The third suggested line of policy will not give us immediate results, but if properly carried out may well in the long run prove of the utmost value in winning the war. Tanks were not introduced because of a military demand; on the contrary, they were imposed on the Army. Their great value was surprise and the absence of any effective counter measure. Now that this element of surprise had been exploited by Germany, effective counter measures for dealing with existing German tanks lie to our hands. But the possession of large numbers of tanks will not of itself constitute a weapon of overwhelming military advantage. If, however, associated with the tanks there were some element of surprise, whether in performance, armaments or even application, then indeed we should be well equipped. I urge, therefore, that tank development as a separate and distinct branch of service be continued. The resource and inventive ability of British engineers are renowned. There is no reason to assume that they cannot do for us in this war what they succeeded in doing in the last.

To these three suggested lines of policy (1) acceleration of existing production (2) rapid augmentation through improvisation, and (3) continuation of development, to which must be added the supplemental aid of purchase from any available source. Given effective direction from the top, our tank position is capable of rapid improvement, but we must have the leadership of men who understand the problem. There is no time to lose.

(In a statement to the House of Commons in December 1942, Churchill admitted that in June 1940 Britain had only a hundred tanks.)

XV

Tanks

One of the gravest defects of Britain's armoured divisions was the lack of technical training of its officers, so that, although the army was now crying out for more and better tanks, it did not know precisely what it should be asking for. The lack of importance given to mechanisation by the high command, typified by many ex-cavalry officers' attitudes to AFVs, meant that the military were unable to give the lead. Luckily, as all motor-car production had come to a halt, there was a supply of experienced civilian talent from that industry which was able to turn its attention to the design of tanks. Over the next two years, in attempts to fill the short-term gap, many different people came up with compromise solutions to the technical difficulties of reconciling gunpower, protection, performance, speed, range of operation and reliability; all problems with which Sam was closely involved.

Sir Albert Stern believed that he could do as well for tanks in this war as he had done in the last and he formed a committee, largely of First World War colleagues, on which Sam was asked to sit. The committee designed a completely new tank (TOG), work on which was carried out by Fosters of Lincoln, Sir William Tritton's firm; but it had many problems and its field trials did not take place until 1943.

Meanwhile, Walter Wilson, with whom Stern was not on very good terms and who declined to join his committee, was busy with the 'surprise element' that Sam had referred to in his speech. He was designing a jet-propelled rocket capable of being fired from a moving vehicle, for use on existing tanks. Since early 1941, when Wilson appealed to him for help, Sam had been trying to get this invention funded but attempts to obtain the materials required for its trials were persistently blocked and his repeated enquiries only yielded the response that the project was 'receiving attention at the highest level'.

For the next two years, Sam was chairman of the unofficial committee of MPs concerned with tanks and worked on a voluntary basis for the Ministry of Supply. Churchill's demands were for greater numbers of tanks; he did not understand the need for better tanks. This, basically meant the Valentine, a light tank, the Matilda and the first Crusaders, all armed with 2-pounder guns. The heavy, slow-moving Matilda tank (later called the Queen of the Desert) provided good protection and was reliable in the early stages against the Italians, but with the arrival of the Germans and their panzer tanks, it proved to be underpowered and under-gunned. After the defeat at Halfaya Pass, reports from North Africa said that all the heavy tanks 'seemed to possess the faults of their predecessors plus quite a few of their own'.

There was a complicated web of organisations responsible for the production of tanks and a gap between their users (the army), their designers, their producers, the Tank Board and the Ministry of Supply. All matters of tank design were in theory under the control of the Department of Tank Design but, under the parentage system, many different private firms either made whole tanks, bits of tanks, or simply assembled them. Sam proposed that more responsibility be given to the parent company for the completion of each type of tank and an engineer be put in charge of design improvement.

One of the design teams was W.A. Robotham's group of ex-Rolls Royce engineers at Belper, which succeeded in putting a modified Merlin engine (a Meteor) into a Crusader and then a Cromwell. Work on the transmission was carried out by Walter Wilson's eldest son,

Gordon. Vickers Armstrong made the Matildas and Vauxhall Motors in Luton were developing the Churchill. Nuffields in Birmingham were making Valentines (also made in Canada) and were developing Convenanters and Crusaders. The Birmingham Railway Carriage & Wagon Co. were the parent company for the Cromwell. Other suppliers were LMS at Crewe, English Electric at Stafford and Leyland Motors at Kingston, all making various parts or getting them from subcontractors. There were at this time 16 different British models, classified by function, whereas the Germans had three basic models.

Sam's angle of expertise was industrial. He complained in the House that the Ministry of Supply was not efficient in organising the arrival of tank parts at the assembly shops; that many tanks being turned out were designed before the war to out-of-date production techniques, and he also asked questions about the production and supply of machine tools. British tanks, he said, were, compared to the Germans, of poor design, of outdated construction, had thin armour and weak guns, and suffered from chronic unreliability.

On 1 July 1941, he spoke in the Central Direction of the War debate, saying that the organisation overlooking the supply of tanks to the army was defective. He based this, he said, on his experience of attending tank trials at which it was clear that the army did not know exactly what it wanted and the Ministry of Supply 'sold' the tanks they were producing without at the same time pointing out their defects. He then went on to say that he would like to express the hope of co-operation from the Admiralty, in connection with what the Prime Minister had said earlier in the debate about the battle in Libya being like a naval battle, with the control of light naval guns comparable to the control of heavy guns in tanks. But he had not, he said, seen any such co-operation. (This speech was reported in the *National Review*.)

Later in this same debate he asked: 'Have we any guns capable of an anti-tank role?' To which he got the rather simplistic reply that the 3.7-inch was the British equivalent of the 88-millimetre and could be used in an anti-tank role. The debate continued with some speakers calling for changes in the Cabinet and others for a change of CIGS (Chief of Imperial General Staff). Churchill, meanwhile, dismissed one after another of the commanders-in chief in North Africa as defeat succeeded defeat.

Sam returned again and again to the question of design reliability. As well as closer co-operation between design departments and manufacturers, he felt that the War Office should co-operate more fully with the suppliers of tanks. Design, he said in a speech in the House, was inclined to be secretive therefore the old mistakes were repeated. 'As we certainly cannot expect to have more tanks than the enemy, we must have better tanks.' He criticised the organisation within the Ministry of Supply, which was in three parts: the Tank Development Board (set up by Lord Beaverbrook to replace the earlier Mechanisation Board), the Stern Committee and private designers of tanks made by private contractors. 'All this organisation is associated with mistakes', he said. After two more speakers the debate went into secret session.

Sam worked closely with Sir Albert Stern often dining with him at the Reform Club or inviting him to Brooks's. He was a forceful character who was at least ten years Sam's senior but as both were determined that the British Army should have better tanks, they got on well together.

In early December, Sam wrote to Erskine-Hill of the 1922 Committee saying: 'the position of tank design and development is causing many people great uneasiness. It is not merely a matter of tanks at present available to the Army, but also the tanks on which we are expected to rely for any major operation in 1942'. He then addressed the 1922 Committee on the subject of tanks, with particular reference to the campaign in North Africa. Here the British had been pushed back to within 70 miles of Alexandria, leaving the desert strewn with tanks that had to be abandoned because of mechanical breakdown. Yet GHQ

Middle East had not formed a Technical Branch until the previous month, November, and no proper tests had been carried out on the range of the German 88-millimetre guns so that, in spite of their heavy armour, the Matilda tanks, had been 'torn to pieces' when the range of the German guns proved greater than anticipated.

The following week Sam led a deputation to Lord Beaverbrook, after which, at the invitation of Sir Frank Newnes, he dined at the latter's house with Beaverbrook, A.G. Elliott, C.J. Radcliffe, the Director General of the Ministry of Information, and Shute of the Air Ministry. Later he had further meetings with Beaverbrook both at the ministry and at Great George Street. Then, just after this, he received a letter from the Ministry of Supply which shows that, at last, there was a greater awareness among those in power of the serious defects in tank gearboxes. 'The gearbox failures i.e. transmission', it read, 'are now colossal, in fact every machine so far produced is suspect on this account alone. To be quite impartial, these gearboxes are not made by Vauxhall but by David Brown, designed I believe by Dr. Merritt, either still or of late, Directorate of Tank Design. But the main failure was due to faulty material.'

Sam did not entirely agree with this. 'It may be that some of the material is faulty', he wrote in a letter to Major B. Bloomer of the Armoured Fighting Vehicles Inspection Branch, dated January 1942, 'but personally I think the design is also faulty'. The letter began with Sam thanking Bloomer for a letter the latter had sent him about the Churchill tank. 'Vauxhalls', he wrote, 'take the view that the suspension is now right. I am not so sanguine. The present chief difficulty is the gear box. I do not know whether you have looked into it, but you will find if you do that the Merritt design involves the use of the gear box in conjunction with the differential steering. The result is that the load on the gear wheel teeth is excessive.' He then wrote to his fellow members of the House of Commons Tank Committee about the position, having spent two days

107

in Birmingham 'checking up on serious information received'.

In a speech he made in the House on 8 January, he set out the history and development of the various tank types, saying 'the submission I have to make to the House is that the mechanical lessons to be learned from our earliest tanks have not been assimilated in our present tanks and that the prospects for future production afford solid grounds for apprehension.' He then criticised the organisation at the Ministry of Supply for not tapping existing expertise. 'I yield to no one', he said, 'in my admiration of the way in which the Prime Minister can flourish a revolver. Let us see that the revolver is loaded.' This speech appeared in *The Spectator* under the heading 'disclosures re. tanks' and there was an article in *The Times* quoting him, followed by letters. However, another letter he wrote to *The Times* was censored on the grounds of 'sensitive material' and was not published.

In March 1942, a trial of the Crusader tank took place at Farnborough to decide whether production should proceed with a (Rolls Royce) Meteor or a (Leyland) Liberty engine. The Meteor engine, which was the Merlin aircraft engine by another name, proved to be much faster than the Liberty and its installation in both Crusader and Cromwell tanks was okayed by Beaverbrook in his famous million-pound telegram to Robotham.

It was not, however, only a fast engine that new cruiser tanks required. Heavy, fast tanks like the Cromwell and the Churchill also called for proper suspension. The construction of suitable gun-turrets was also necessary for the use of more powerful guns (75-millimetre guns could be supplied by the Americans). The British General Staff had always had armour-plate bolted or riveted onto their tank hulls, greatly adding to the weight, yet the Germans had been welding armour-plate since before the war. All these problems were thrown at the design teams, none of whose personnel had experience of military vehicles.

Throughout this whole period Sam expressed his anxiety

– 'my very great anxiety' – about the future of tank development and repeatedly attacked the organisation in charge. 'This', he said, 'is unsatisfactory largely because it ignores both the knowledge which exists and those people who possess the knowledge'. He did not, he said, want to say anything of assistance to the enemy but it was particularly the mechanical defects in tanks that he was anxious about. He asked if any of the latest type of tank (the Churchill) had been sent to Libya and, if so, what were the reports of their mechanical reliability? He urged that 'a small executive tank board, sitting day by day' be set up, 'consisting of a Chairman, a Director of Design & Development, a Director of Production and a War Office representative who should be a member of the Army Council in touch with the Tank Users Committee.' He justified the 'late hour' (after 10 p.m.) at which he was making this speech by saying that it was a matter of urgency.

He also argued that the proper use of available manpower was central to the successful conduct of the war and in March he spoke in the House about overmanning at the newly constituted Ministry of Production. He also appealed again for more manufacturing support and organisation of labour in connection with 'the complex engineering problems of tank production'. Although he was not trained as an engineer, he carried on a voluminous technical correspondence on such things as suspension, gearboxes and gear-selector-forks as problems persisted and throughout this period was in touch with many engineering firms. He co-operated with Colonel D.T. Raikes, who was a tank production inspector at the War Office, whom he knew from the Tanks Corps in the First World War; he attended trials of the 25-pounder gun on a Loyd Carrier; wrote about alternative suspension for the Churchill tank and went to Lincoln for the trials of a gyro-stabilised gun intended for the Stern Committee's 80-ton tank, 'The Old Gang'.

Guy Dowding, who had written to Sam earlier in the year about the shortage of rollers for bearings of tank-steering units seriously affecting output, wrote to him again after the fall of Tobruk, (June 1942): 'In this latest defeat we have again been out-ranged and out-gunned. Will this crisis be the means, at last, of getting rid of the incompetent team [Tank Board] who are responsible for these repeated failures to produce tanks and anti-tank equipment?'

Both Sam and Richard Stokes had for some time been asking questions in the House designed to cause embarrassment to the Tank Board, which was considered by all those who had to deal with it to be both obstructive and overmanned and whose Director General was highly unpopular. When eventually something was done, Sam asked a further question. 'Is the House to understand', he asked, 'that the Director General of the Tank Board, who for so many months has protected and defended the delinquencies of officers with whom he has been working, has now decided that it is right and proper that they should go and that he should remain?'

However, when the Director General, Oliver Lucas, was replaced, he was sent to America on a tank mission! Edward Keeling, Sam's colleague on the Parliamentary Tank Committee, warned the House that he was not the man to be sent, and the British Embassy in Washington wrote that he would not be acceptable to the Americans. Stokes asked for a secret debate so that he could reveal the information that he had concerning him which would 'astonish the House'. But W.A. Robotham, who had joined the Ministry of Supply as Controller-General of (Tank) Research & Development in 1941, at Beaverbrook's request, got on well with Oliver Lucas. Robotham described him as more interested in things mechanical than he was in people and praised him for the support he gave to the work that was being done on tanks by his (Robotham's) research team of ex-Rolls Royce engineers at Belper. By 1943, however, further misunderstandings caused Robotham to resign from the Ministry and have nothing further to do with tanks; and Richard Stokes,

110

speaking during another debate, in July, at which a vote of censure was taken, reported that the atmosphere at the Tank Board was such that Lucas's successor, A. Boyd, 'did not last long but returned to his firm, leaving in complete disgust'.

XVI

David Brown

Problems relating to the production of tanks and the machine tools necessary for their manufacture occupied Sam throughout the war. He was particularly concerned with controls and distribution from within the Ministry of Supply, asking questions about the numbers of British and American machine tools in store and about bottlenecks in the supply of jigs. In February 1942 Lord Beaverbrook asked him to visit Vauxhall Motors in Luton, as a follow-up to the Ministry of Supply's letter to him in connection with the trouble that Vauxhalls were having with the tank gearboxes being supplied to them from David Brown & Sons.

The combined works of David Brown & Sons (Huddersfield) and David Brown & Sons (Tractors), with their subsidiaries, was the chief supplier of the Merritt-Brown gearbox, designed by Dr H.E. Merritt (adviser to the Department of Tank Design from 1939 until the Tank Board was formed in May 1940). Their output was, therefore, vital to the British war effort. Vauxhalls were engaged in the production of Mark IV Churchill tanks.

After the visit, which Sam made with Walter Wilson and Kit's brother Jeff as engineering support, the Chairman of the Tank Board received the following letter from the Managing Director of Vauxhalls, C.J. Bartlett:

I told Mr Hammersley that the general character of the problem was that we were asking a firm – David Brown & Sons – to go into what was virtually mass

112

production on gear boxes, and that David Brown & Sons had really no experience of this kind of work whatsoever. They had no experience of setting down limits and tolerances, which are necessary in repetition work, relying on 'Old Bill' or 'Old George' skimming a bit here or fitting a bit there. There was at David Brown's perhaps rather an inclination to feel that they knew of these things and that they could soon put them right if only people would let them do 'an engineering job' in their own way.

In June the Ministry of Supply appointed Sam Managing Director of David Brown & Sons, putting him on the board with two other nominees, T.C. Gutherie and R. Officer, to replace four existing directors. David Brown, although he remained as Chairman, was not pleased. He insisted that there was to be no interference with share structures and no merging of the Huddersfield and Meltham factories, and he encouraged his directors to resist being replaced, so that they had to be deposed through solicitors.

The firm was an old-established one, proud of its traditions, and Sam had a hard fight trying to change working practices, install a system of close inspection to ensure the laid-down tolerances were adhered to, and make sure that all machines were used to capacity. The policy statement that he drew up was designed to involve the whole workforce in increasing production and said that the company should 'seek out ability and initiative in the ranks', 'provide an assured ladder of promotion' and 'encourage the higher executives to exert the maximum influence over the affairs of the company'. This David Brown construed as a direct threat to his own authority and from the very start he undermined attempts to implement it.

Tensions between him and his permanent staff on the one hand and the ministry nominees on the other soon manifested themselves and, although a courtesy car was always sent to collect Sam from the Clarendon Club in Manchester to bring him to the board meetings, it soon became clear that Sam's policy was not being carried out. Neither he nor his colleagues were being given free access to the works managers and they did not think that the attitude of the Secretary, who was a personal financial adviser to Mr Brown, was impartial.

During this time, Sam's diary shows that he attended tank tests at Brooklands, followed by numerous meetings at the Ministry of Supply (Shell Mex House), the War Office and the Ministry of Production. Throughout the summer reports were coming in that tank gearboxes were still overheating and that Crusader tanks were leaking oil. This, Sam felt, was not so much a failure of the gearbox as of the basic design of the tanks for which the gearbox was intended.

In July there was a vote of censure in the House and, just before the battle of El Alamein, the Minister of Defence toured the fighting units in the Middle East, returning with the pessimistic report that 'there were, alas, no weapons adequate for the fight'. Nevertheless, the British were victorious at El Alamein, which can now be seen as a turning point in the war. A later debate in the House of Commons, on 11 November, however, showed that anxiety about armaments had not been allayed. A small number of Churchill tanks had taken part in the battle but it was primarily the Shermans that had proved so valuable. Had not some 300 of these, together with 100 105-millimetre self-propelled guns, been sent to Egypt by the Americans for the build-up of the 8th Army, the outcome could quite well have been different.

During the November debate there were several voices raised in protest about the tank position. F. Cocks (Broxtowe) asked: 'Why is it that America has been able to produce a first-class tank whereas Great Britain after three years of war has not been able to do so? Those responsible for this outrageous carelessness and incompetence should be punished.'

Commander Sir Archibald Southby (Epsom) said that he would have greater confidence in the future if he could be assured that 'those responsible for glaring defects in tanks and other things had been removed from their job', and T.I. Horabin (Cornwall North), who had earlier had a meeting with Sam, declared that 'the defects in our tanks which prevented us winning in Libya earlier were qualitative, not quantitative. Those defects were due to a failure to plan effectively; the plain facts of the matter are that the British tanks of 1942 were not battleworthy. They had guns with too short range; there were mechanical defects due to bad design and we had no hope of victory in Libya, as the Prime Minister told us, until we were assured of adequate supplies of the American Sherman tank. I think the present situation as regards tank design is a scandal.'

Although the taking of El Alamein had kept the Germans out of Egypt, it was not until May of 1943, after the Americans had landed in Morocco and the British had landed new forces in Tunisia and Algeria, that the Germans were finally driven out of the whole of North Africa; by which time, although Churchill tanks were becoming available in greater numbers, the German forces had been equipped with Tiger tanks with 88-millimetre guns, the design of which was greatly superior to anything British. When Richard Stokes pressed the Secretary of State for War to say if the British tanks coming into production were superior to the German and Sir James Grigg (Secretary of State for War) had answered that in his opinion they would be, Richard answered to much laughter, 'well you are wrong.'

On 16 February 1943, an article appeared in the *Evening Standard*, written by Sam, with the title 'Victory Tank'. In it he set out, for the general public, the features that would be required for a new heavy tank and explained the difficulties there were in reconciling the need for more speed with the need for heavier armour and greater firepower, as well as the difficulties with mechanical transmission systems in maintaining the tractive effort of the engine, particularly

115

when changing speed in lower gears.

Sam's position at David Brown's was getting worse rather than better. In January 1943 he wrote a report to the Ministry of Supply and Aircraft Production (also signed by Gutherie and Officer) 'in view of the deadlock which has now arisen in the direction of the affairs of David Brown Ltd'. In it they listed the problems they were having, under two headings: 'Management' and 'Production', stating that the chief one was with David Brown himself who, they wrote, 'does not manage; he calls for reports and dictates policy. His chief anxiety is to stand between the Board and the Management in order to see that his policy is imposed on the company. Production is, to Mr Brown, quite a secondary consideration.' Under the second heading, 'Production', they wrote: 'our method has been, firstly to ascertain the facts, secondly to diagnose the source of weakness and thirdly to direct the attention of those normally responsible to the need for improvement. In every case these improvements have been forthcoming, *though the utmost firmness has been required to get Mr Brown to act.*' They concluded: 'the independent members of the Board are unanimously of the opinion that Mr David Brown is not a suitable person to be in control of an organisation engaged in the manufacture of vital key production requirements for the prosecution of the war.'

When significant improvements in production were achieved at two of the subsidiary companies in the David Brown Group, David Brown could not accept that this was due to interventions by Sam or either of his colleagues, and when Sam proposed that the manager of one of these works, Mr Rowe, be made Joint Managing Director with him on the main board, David Brown vigorously opposed it. He then wrote a long report to the ministries, refuting what had been said against him, which he got his works managers to support in writing, making the position of Sam and the other two independents quite untenable. Since the production figures of all the companies in the group had been steadily improving, *even before the indepen-*

116

dent managers were appointed, it was impossible to prove, disprove or quantify the extent to which they had contributed. In March 1943, they all resigned.

In that same month, Sam wrote an article for *The Spectator* with the title 'Heavy Tanks'. He had recently met Captain Frederick Erroll (later to be an MP and receive a baronetcy) who was working in a technical capacity in connection with tank construction and testing. He was an MIEE and AMIMechE and had worked before the war at Metropolitan-Vickers Electrical in Manchester. Although only 28 when Sam was 50, they became good friends, and Freddy acknowledged later that Sam was of great help to him throughout his career. They had first met during tests on the Cromwell tank and thereafter worked together closely. Erroll often stayed at Saxons.

When in October Sam wrote another article for *The Spectator*, this time entitled 'The Essential Tank', in which, as an illustration of inaccuracy, he had referred to the use of an 'eclectic yardstick', Freddy sent him a facetious letter. 'None of my engineering friends', he wrote, 'seems to know what an "eclectic yardstick' is or what units it measures in. Perhaps it is ignorance of this apparently useful device which is the cause of our "out-tankation", if I may coin a phrase.'

Sam continued his watchdog activities for the Parliamentary Tank Committee and kept up his contacts with the army and the Ministries of Supply and of Production. He visited the Army AFV School at Bovington, where, among others, he contacted an old friend from Littlestone, Colonel Loup; and a diary entry shows that he was there again a month later. He also visited the Inspectorate of Fighting Vehicles at Chislehurst, at the invitation of Commander E.R. Micklem, its Director. Later in 1943 he attended the comparative trials (called Operation Dracula) at Bovington where two types of American Sherman tanks were compared with the British Cromwell and Centaur. The results of the trial favoured the Shermans, which showed exemplary reliability, while the

117

British cruisers needed constant attention.

The frequent changes in the composition of the Tank Board influenced the British General Staff to rely increasingly on American supplies, although an efficient British cruiser tank could have been on stream in time had proper support been given to the engineers at Belper. Their success in mounting the Meteor engine in a Cromwell, which gave it speeds well in excess of those of the Sherman, was not appreciated although, space-wise, it was interchangeable with the Liberty engine and they had the prototype ready by 1942. W.A. Robotham resigned from the Ministry of Supply in August 1943 when the project to put a 17-pounder gun in a Sherman, rather than into the Challenger on which he was working and which he considered more suitable, was given the go-ahead against his technical advice.

When the House reassembled in September there was still a feeling that the British army had no choice but to rely on American Sherman tanks. Sam asked why there should be a wasteful duplication of British resources producing inferior tanks 'in view of the large supplies of efficient American tanks now regularly arriving in this country' and, in another debate in early November, he again raised the matter by asking about co-ordination in tank production between Britain and the USA. Both he and Edward Keeling also asked questions of the Minister of Production in connection with the tank programme. Keeling wanted to know what changes had been made to the Tank Board, getting a written reply which showed that, although Mr Oliver Lucas still sat on it, it was now under the chairmanship of Commander Micklem. But both he and Richard Stokes continued with questions about the composition of the Board of Tank Development & Design (particularly the Director), with whom none of them was satisfied, calling for a statement on tank production 'in view of the great anxiety which exists in the House on this matter'.

In December Sam produced a (secret) document on 'The Present Position of British Tank Production' in which he dealt with tanks of the Cromwell group (Cromwell, Crusader, Challenger and Comet), which were to be Britain's answer to the German panzers. In this he discussed mechanical reliability, firepower, protection and speed, and concluded that, unless it was fitted with a 95-millimetre gun, the Cromwell should be scrapped. His frequent questions in the House about gun calibres and weight of armament of the tanks then being committed in the Sicilian campaign and later on the mainland of Italy, were a constant embarrassment to the ministry. Yet the War Office had continued, ever since the Tripoli victory in February 1943, to think in terms of the desert experience when considering what tanks were required, although the terrain in Europe, where they now had to operate, was so different.

In bringing to light the deficiencies of British tanks, care had to be taken not to give encouragement to the enemy. However, when the House of Commons went into secret session on 24 March 1944, Sam was able to make the following speech:

The case I have to submit to the House is that well over £200 million have been spent on the production of British tanks and that in this fifth year of the war there are no British tanks available to the Army which in either striking power, protection or mechanical reliability are equal to the best tanks of the enemy. We have not produced a reliable tank transmission. It was the American Sherman tank which prevented us being out-tanked in North Africa. It was the American Sherman tank which was used in Sicily. It is the American Sherman tank which is being used in Italy now. We are at the present time completely dependent on American tank production, yet British tanks are still being manufactured. A huge organisation of tank design, production and inspection is in being. Scores of works, hundreds of thousands of men are engaged. Materials are converted. Millions

119

are spent. What has the country got from this effort? What are our fighting men getting today?

Sam's diary shows that he and Richard Stokes had been meeting regularly since 1942, and in 1944 the latter came several times to Sam's Chesham Street flat and also spent a weekend at Saxons. When in April 1943 the government had allowed it to be known that the Centaur tank was being taken off the Secret List, which was a public admission that it was no good, between them they gave the Prime Minister and the Minister of Supply 'a very hard time' in the House. Yet production was not stopped. Both the Centaur and the Cromwell were to be continued, although the new Comet and Centurion (the ultimate tank of World War II) were both more powerful and were already coming on stream.

However, in spite of his worries about the quality of our tanks, in October 1943 Sam made a speech in his constituency in which he prophesied: 'The war will be won, although not yet. We are nearer the end than the start.'

Sam and Kit on the beach, 1918

Sam's election photograph, 1923

Christening of Jenniver Œnone in crypt of House of Commons, 1930. Sam, Joan Birch, Kit, Oliver Baldwin, Lavender Dower, Priscilla, Nanny with Baby, Barbara Jill, Penelope

Sam's election photo, 1950

Delta Mill

Lily Mill

Sam and Kit at Saxon Court with their grandchildren, 1958

Sam in 1962

XVII

Conduct of the War

When there is a national government and therefore no official opposition, as throughout the war, it is the duty of all backbenchers to challenge the government without consideration of party advantage. Although most of Sam's speeches and questions during this period were concerned with tank production, he continued to be interested in industrial affairs generally and particularly in monetary policy. He often started a speech by saying that he spoke 'from the producer's point of view', and in 1941, he introduced his speech on the need to divert workers from non-essential trades to war production with 'each of us has an individual contribution to make to the successful conclusion of this war, mine is based on considerable and close industrial experience.'

This was the speech, quoted in *The Economist*, in which he contended that compulsion and compensation was proceeding well with large concerns, but Concentration of Production orders were not being applied to small businesses. In cotton, some 40 per cent of capacity was now closed down or closing down, he said, (his own Rex Mill was closed, only starting up again in 1948) 'but it was small businesses which before the war were responsible for the bulk of the total production of the country'. He gave the example, with figures, of a typical non-essential small industry. He also cited the retail trade as a clear-cut case of untapped manpower. 'Coercion and compensation,' he urged, 'should be applied to all non-essential trades.'

When he spoke in the Budget debate in 1941, he accused

the Chancellor of being over-afraid of inflation 'when the only question he should be asking himself was: does it [the measure] do everything possible to further the waging of the war?' In this same debate, he spoke again of the need for labour to be organised, but at the same time he pressed for the imposition of a capital levy, saying that equity of sacrifice called for a co-ordinated policy, not only on work and wages but also on taxation.

In the 1942 Budget debate, he congratulated the Chancellor on imposing income tax on weekly wage-earners and on the new allowances for married women. However, he argued that reduction of income tax for the middle classes was the best way to safeguard the capitalist system after the war and he foresaw the probability of talented youth going overseas if industry was deprived of capital. 'Government and industry', he said, 'must get together if exports are to flourish after the war'.

In February 1943 he wrote an article for the *Manchester Evening News* entitled 'Cotton's Future in a Revival of Exports' and wrote to *The Times* on the subject of the vertical linking of mill and merchant so as to ensure the economical use of machinery on long runs. This letter was quoted in the *New English Review*.

In the committee stage of the Budget debate he called for a new clause to alter the base on which Excess Profits Tax was calculated in order to alleviate the position of depressed industries, arguing that, by removing the phrase 'at that date', businesses which had reorganised before the war, reducing capital, would have their tax more equitably assessed. He also asked about compensatory EPT payments for firms that were prepared to contract because of war requirements, proposing lower income tax 'in respect of undistributed profits'. He then returned to his proposal for a capital levy, saying: 'Total war demands the use of all our resources; this includes capital as well as income.'

In May he made a speech in the House saying that cotton-mill plant should be written down on the basis of its replacement value, not on its old value. Just as between the wars he had urged government to intervene to raise cotton prices now, in changed circumstances, he urged it to keep them down. 'In the cotton trade', he said, 'we have a Controller but no control. The result is disastrous. For the first time in twenty years demand exceeds supply. There is profit-taking and spiralling wages. Prices in the cotton trade ought to be controlled'.

Throughout the war Sam spent a good deal of his time in East Willesden making himself 'available to constituents' as his diary puts it, addressing meetings and appearing at functions. He was also an active member of the Tory Reform Group, in which he took part in discussions about the need there was going to be for more social security when troops were demobilised. Like Harold Macmillan and others of the same generation who had seen the mass unemployment at the end of the First World War, he was very much aware of its dangers and throughout his life tempered his Conservatism with humanitarian considerations. He also discussed this with Dick Law but, although the latter had been in the United States during the Depression, he put his faith in 'market forces' and did not share Sam's fears.

In the Budget debates in 1943 Sam spoke on the proposals for an improved international monetary mechanism. 'There is an American proposal put forward and a British proposal', he said. 'Let us concentrate on the similarities. Neither is intended to be a complete panacea but both are preferable to the rigidity of the Gold Standard.' He gave a simple exposé for post-war international finance, referring to the British plan as the Keynes plan, likening the proposed new monetary institution to a shop 'where countries who trade can obtain an overdraft of a fixed amount and in which the goods that are on sale – foreign exchange – are marked up in plain terms'. The quotas in each of the plans were differently arrived at but the goal was the same. In the US plan they were to be gold and foreign exchange holdings, and in the Keynes

123

plan, imports and exports. Sam favoured relating the quotas to the fluctuations in the balance of payments, but both plans, he said, were at the tentative stage and we should try for a solution agreeable to both. These proposals culminated in the inauguration of the International Monetary Fund at Bretton Woods in July 1944.

The year 1943 had started with Churchill, Roosevelt and Stalin meeting at the Casablanca Conference and agreeing to postpone a landing in northern Europe, starting the Italian campaign instead and, shortly afterwards, a bomber offensive against Germany. When they next met, in November in Tehran, concessions were made to Stalin, confirmed later at Yalta, which condemned Poland, as well as most of the rest of Eastern and Central Europe, to years of Soviet domination, although Poland had more squadrons fighting with the RAF than all the other Allies combined and Polish army divisions were fighting with the British and Americans in Italy.

In May 1943 Albert Kohan (who had taken the Resistance name of Berthaud) was flown to London by the Free French Government. He brought his current mistress, Victoria, with him and they stayed together in a tiny flat, found by Sam close to his own in Chesham Street, coming down to Saxons for weekends. Sam gave a big dinner at the Dorchester for him, Colonel Passy and others of his London superiors from Duke Street. Albert was responsible for setting up the liberation movement in Nice, Marseilles and Lyon, and now the Free French Government wanted him to remain in London to oversee the organisation of another group in the west of France. But Albert refused to stay and, although at least 55 years old, insisted on being parachuted back into France so that he could personally organise the new group himself.

In December the Free French brought him to London again, airlifting him out. He was due to arrive on 17th December and he and Victoria were expected at Saxons for Christmas. But the plane crash-landed in fog and everyone was killed. All through the war, in Occupied

124

France, Albert had taken no precautions to hide himself from the Nazis, in spite of being a Jew and having a memorable face, accent and personality. He survived great risks. He galvanised everyone into believing, as he did, even at the darkest hour, that the Allies would ultimately triumph and had not hesitated to involve his daughter Marion and her husband Claude, who took the Resistance surname Legendre. His short biography in the book of the 'Compagnons de la Libération' says of his death: '*Ainsi disparaissait une des plus belles figures de la France Libre.*'

Two Polish names first appeared in the Saxon Court visitors' book at this time: Bernard Poloniecki, a Polish pilot with the RAF, and George (L.G.) Polturak who, having lost a leg in a car-racing accident, had a Polish Government job in London. Both were from Lwow. After the war L.G., who had an engineering degree, worked for Sam at S. Noton Ltd. so did his brother Felix. L.G. married Vivien Bennett, Barbara Jill's great friend who was in the ATS with her. Earlier in 1943 Barbara Jill had been gassed during an exercise in which an army sergeant sent a platoon of ATS girls into a shed (as training for fire-fighting) where he had started a fire not, as he supposed, with a smoke bomb but with a gas canister. Several of the girls were detained in St George's Hospital and Sam, speaking in the House, asked for an enquiry.

Sam spent a lot of time in his clubs, especially during the war when he was alone in London without Kit. He liked clubs and was a member of both Brooks's and the Carlton, as well as the Clarendon in Manchester. He found them useful for entertaining his business associates and parliamentary colleagues, as well as Manchester friends such as Fred Dehn who, his diary shows, often lunched with him at Brooks's, as did London friends like Simon Harcourt-Smith, Bob Boothby and Harvey Combe, who invited him in turn to their clubs. Albert Stern often dined with him at Brooks's or he went to his clubs, the Reform or the Garrick. Sam also liked to go dancing. The Anthony

Edens liked it too. They all frequented the Dorchester Hotel because it had a good band and a big dance floor. But during air-raids or when the House was sitting late, they went to nightclubs, like the Coconut Grove and the Four Hundred, where the tiny basement dance floors would be crammed with service personnel on leave.

The build-up for 'Overlord' (the invasion of Europe) was by now well under way but, as the whole of Britain had for some time been one armed camp, it was not apparent. Even those involved did not realise that their movements and concentrations were leading up to D-Day. At Saxons a unit of French Canadians were camped in the stables and the paddock. Ruth the cook, a young local girl, was made pregnant by one of them but Kit spoke to the commanding officer and Ruth was married just before the unit left for Normandy. A 'second front' had been long awaited, much anticipated and so often postponed that when it did come it was not only the Germans who were taken by surprise. Bombing raids over Germany had been going on for months, in retaliation for the bombing of British cities, and Kit, who was a light sleeper, had been hearing planes pass over Saxons night and morning, for months. It was only when Churchill (after first telling the House of Commons of the capture of Rome) announced the Normandy landings that ordinary people realised, with jubilation, that at last the second front had opened.

Only a week later, on 13 June, the first V1s started coming over. They were pilotless aircraft (doodlebugs) with the engines set to cut out when over London. But many stopped over Kent and Sussex and one landed in a field next to Saxons and another in Sam's wood. Kit, Sam felt, needed a break and he asked Bernard Poloniecki, who was stationed at Chivenor in Devon, if he could find a house where she could stay with Nanny and the children. They left in June and Sam sent Margaret Allen, his London housekeeper, to join them, partly to get her away from the doodlebugs (thousands of people were leaving London) and partly to do the cooking for Kit. Sarah

126

Macmillan, who joined them in Devon, and Jenniver (both aged 14) fell in love with Bernard and his Polish Air Force colleagues, whom they watched flying over on bombing exercises and who were frequent visitors at the house. McKenzie stayed at Saxon Court, looking after Sam when he joined his daughter Priscilla for weekends.

The doodlebugs were followed, in September, by the V2s. These were ballistic missiles of the same nature as Walter Wilson's rocket, concerning which Sam had just received a letter from the Ministry of Aircraft Production, rejecting it as a 'fruitless expenditure of time and effort'. Simon Harcourt-Smith traced 'Major Wilson's unhappy story' and Sam's efforts on his behalf in an article in the *Sunday Dispatch*, with the title: 'A Flying Bomb *WE* Might Have Had'. The government, however, did not acknowledge these weapons as a new development until eight weeks after they started coming over and more than a hundred had already landed on London. Together with the V1s, they continued to threaten London and the south-east until March 1945.

After Walter Wilson's death in 1957, Sam wrote to the Editor of *The Times* to fill a gap in his published obituary:

There is no mention of his inventive genius during the Second World War yet his ingenious mind was constantly at work in his country's service and who knows what the result might have been had he been given adequate encouragement. Early in 1941 he put forward in considerable detail a proposal for the development of a self-propelled, self-controlled, airborne projectile. When he found himself unable to make progress with the authorities he came to me and over a considerable period of time, on his behalf, I had interviews with Lord Charwell, the Minister of Aircraft Production, Lord Brabazon and the subsequent Minister of Aircraft Production, Sir Stafford Cripps. Summarised, their verdict was that this country had not the resources to bring the project to a successful conclusion in time to vitally affect the War. I do not think that Walter Wilson would necessarily have quarrelled with this conclusion which, after prolonged argument he was forced to accept, but it is worth while recording that several years before this country was afflicted by V1 and V2 missiles, their production had been suggested and their advent predicted by him.

In the summer of 1944 Sam gave himself a week's holiday and joined his family in Devon. (Kit's identity card shows that she and the children did not return to Saxon Court until the end of September.)' Attempts to help the Poles in Warsaw, who had risen against the Germans, were proving very difficult. They were out of practical range of air support from England or Italy and the Allied armies had not yet crossed the Rhine. General Sir John Hackett, who commanded at the battle of Arnhem, wrote in *The Times* that the division of Europe for nearly 50 years 'was the direct result of our failure to capture the bridgehead. If we had been able to get the British Second Army across the Rhine and into the Ruhr, the war would have been over. At the time we were much nearer Berlin than the Russians. If we had got there first, the whole subsequent history of Europe and the Cold War would have been very different'. As for the Russians, although only just across the Vistula, they did nothing to prevent the Germans from reducing Warsaw to a heap of rubble.

Bernard Poloniecki and George Polturak spent Christmas at Saxon Court and by the end of the year Bernard and Barbara Jill were married. Sam did not enjoy the wedding. It was a very cold day and he had not been well and had pains in his wounded leg. Besides, as Kit put it: 'he was like the Grand Turk with his harem and hated parting with his daughters.' However, by the first days of 1945 he had sufficiently recovered to take advantage of parliamentary privilege and go over to Paris, in a Dakota, with his friend and colleague Edward

Keeling. He wrote a short note to Kit saying: 'everyone in uniform, including K. Had lunch with Claude and Marion [Legendre] and then to the races at Longchamps.'

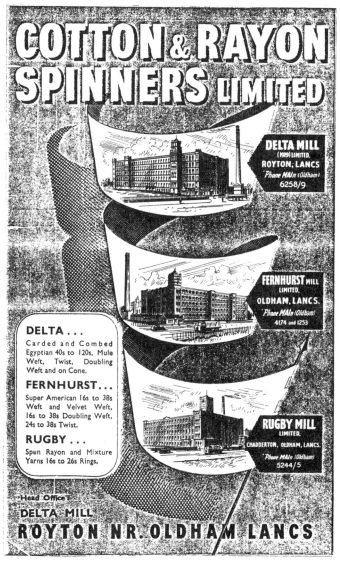

XVIII

Threads of Peace

In May 1945 the Germans capitulated, agreeing to 'unconditional surrender', and the war in Europe was over. While Lady Churchill was promoting 'Aid to Russia', millions had been spent by the Soviet Union on Communist propaganda, both in the forces and the factories. Few British people knew how far the idealistic society pictured by this propaganda differed from the reality of life in the USSR. But in any case, everyone, having fought together, dug for victory together, been bombed together, rationed together and generally involved in the make-do-and-mend of the war together, wanted a more egalitarian society. They needed little encouragement to vote Labour when the Labour Party was backing Beveridge's Social Insurance Plan and talking of nationalising the hospitals.

The general election held in July 1945 was the first since 1937. Sam's election pamphlet had a photograph of his youngest daughter, Philippa, with 'One Generation to Another' and 'What does the Future Hold for YOU – HER?' on the front. And on the back: 'HAMMERSLEY The Man * Who knows the ropes of parliament, * Who knows the problems of the Ex-service Man and Woman, * Who has a Forward View, * Who knows the value of Home Life, * Who is out to build a better Britain.' He was, however, defeated by the same Maurice Orbach, an avowed Communist, who had stood against him in 1938. The Tories were ousted throughout the country in a landslide Labour victory and Churchill, who had for so long been the country's inspiration, although he kept his own seat, was no longer Prime Minister.

Failing to be re-elected was not, therefore, so bitter a blow for Sam as it might have been since so many of his former colleagues were also defeated. (Richard Law lost Kingston upon Hull and Harold Macmillan lost Stockton on Tees). Sir David Maxwell-Fyfe, however, who had been Recorder for Oldham from 1936 until he was made Solicitor-General in 1942, managed to keep Liverpool.

Maxwell-Fyfe was Sam's friend and neighbour in Sussex, and visited Saxons with his daughters. Having been appointed Deputy Chief Prosecutor at the Nuremberg Trials, he was obliged to sit in judgement on the Nazis, who were accused not only of all the terrible crimes against humanity they really did commit but also of the murder of Polish officers in the Katyn forest. When the Polish Government in London protested, saying that Katyn was a crime committed by the Soviet Union, Stalin cynically used the incident to break off relations with it. (The guilt for Katyn, together with the murder of other Polish officers in other Russian camps, which was a deliberate attempt to deprive the Polish nation of its educated élite, was not acknowledged until the fall of the Soviet regime.)

With the demobilisation of British forces, the Labour Government sent all Polish servicemen a letter, signed by the Foreign Secretary, Ernest Bevin, strongly urging them to return home. But members of a breakaway pro-Communist government who left London for Poland were put on trial in Moscow, imprisoned and then sent to the *gulags*; and the worst fears of the Free Poles were confirmed when members of the armed forces who had fought on the side of the Allies went back to Poland and were treated in the same way, as spies and traitors, and sent to Siberia or executed.

With the termination of war with Japan, Lend-Lease which had supplied Britain with food as well as armaments on credit, was brought to an end and the Labour Government was forced to reduce rations. (Rationing continued

131

at this low level until 1949 and did not end completely until 1954.) Sam responded to the continuing food shortages by taking on an extra gardener to step up the production of fruit and vegetables from the walled kitchen garden at Saxon Court, which he sold through East Sussex Growers.

He had not seen a lot of his relations during the war years. His diary shows only one appointment with his sister Gladys, when he took her to the Berkeley Hotel for lunch on her birthday in 1941. She had lived in Sussex ever since she returned from Vienna in 1937 but with continuing petrol rationing, she could not easily get over to Saxon Court. Her daughter, Joanna who had married Denis Ryland in 1939, now had two small children, Merrylees and Gyles. She had stayed a few days in Sam's London flat, before she was married, and remembers how he was most insistent that she be in by midnight. 'I think,' she said, 'he thought I was out of control and felt guilty that he had not been more of a guardian to me.'

Sam's younger sister, Constance, and her husband, John Snell, lived in Southport with their children, David and Rosalind. Sam stayed with them sometimes when he was in the north, instead of going to his club. He had lunched with Ronald Hardman, his cousin Hilda's husband, at the Clarendon Club in Manchester in 1941 and in 1942 his cousin Doreen Hamer came to lunch at his 19 Chesham Street flat. The Hammersley connections had been lucky; unlike so many families, they had not been split up by the war and only one Schofield relation, Terence Russell, who stayed a few days at Saxons in 1940, had been killed.

Sam, who was always fussy about his food, his clothes and his personal hygiene, had not put up with wartime austerity gladly. But although he was anxious for life at Saxons to return to a peacetime footing as soon as possible, this was not easy. The days of reliable living-in servants were over and the maids' rooms at the top of the house, which had last been used for the evacuees, were empty. McKenzie retired to a flat near Hurlingham, claiming the units of utility furniture to which rationing entitled her and taking as much care of them as she had of Kit's antiques. Over the next few years, she returned to Saxons for short periods but, after breaking her hip, left for good, going to an old people's home in her native Nairn. Nanny continued to provide a haven in the nursery, where Jenniver, Philippa and Kit would have their supper during the week when Sam was away. But, although Kit liked the simple life, she never ate in the kitchen and at weekends, helped by local girls, she and Sam had weekend guests again and entertained.

Martin and Andrew Law, who had returned from the States with American accents, came with their parents, ribbing their father (whose last job in Churchill's National Government had been Minister of State) by calling him 'Old Stately'. Martin was sad that they no longer had their country house, Dolloways, as this had been the 'home' he conjured up all the while he was away. But they had moved back to London in 1944, just before Dick had been sent, with John Maynard Keynes, to Bretton Woods for the setting up of the International Monetary Fund.

Natasha Cruthers also returned from America and redeemed her emerald. Philip Noel-Baker, who was Minister of State in the Labour Government, and his wife Irene spent a weekend talking about the situation in Greece, which Yalta had confirmed as a British area of influence. Here the government was waging war on the Communists and their son, Francis, had gone to reclaim the property at Achmetaga that Lord Byron had given to Irene's grandfather.

Geoffrey Lowis was demobbed from the navy and Lallie Lee returned from America with their children. But the Lowis marriage was on the rocks, the years of war when they had been separated making reconciliation difficult. Geoffrey wrote to Kit in an undated letter:

I thought you had patched up our leaky ship the other

133

day and nearly wrote my gratitude. Then she went off on the loose with her drinking companions and reverted to her old morose condition. However, for one day she was a charming companion again and even took an interest in my navvy work in the garden – which I strongly suspect you put her up to. I am beginning to think she might be happier with someone else who would adapt himself 100% to doing what she wants to do. After six years with only the strain of war to bear I am not tolerating strains at home. Which probably makes me a rather uncongenial mate. Love and don't give up.

Then at the bottom of the letter, which was typed, he wrote: 'See you Saturday but we shall have no opportunity for you to tell me not to be a fool.'

Just before Christmas 1946 Sam and Geoffrey went over to Ireland together for a week's shooting. Sam also shot with his friend John Stourton, who had been in the House with him and now lived at Wadhurst. Sam and John both enjoyed a joke. But when Sam, intrigued by Existentialism, wrote a note about 'Sartre laughing at the Peace Conference' it was only half in fun; he was disillusioned both by the stupidity of 'unconditional surrender' and by the Nuremberg Trials. Geoffrey and Lallie divorced and a few years later Geoffrey married again.

Sam was pleased that he already had grandchildren; it was the next best thing for him to having a baby of his own. Penelope's eldest two, Toby and Charlotte, had been born at Saxons with a resident maternity nurse. But the arrangement was not repeated for any other grandchildren as Sam now felt that, with so little help in the house, it would be too much for Kit. Neither was he prepared to put up with the inconvenience of young children running all over the place. He got very angry and very red in the face when they disobeyed him.

After the outside broadcasting section of the BBC that had operated throughout the war from the Eckersleys' house near Eridge moved back to London, Pen and Tim (Eckersley) bought a house close to Saxons. In the summer of 1946 they lost their third child, Tabitha, at the age of four months; when her mother went out to the pram to bring her in for her lunch, she found her dead. There is a photograph of her in Penelope's lap, taken at Saxons shortly before, with Toby, Charlotte and her Poloniecki cousin, Jan. At that time 'cot deaths' were not widely publicised and everyone was terribly shocked. The Laws arranged a holiday in Cornwall for Penelope and Timothy at a seaside cottage they had rented before buying their farm, Boccadon.

Having got in for South Kensington at a by-election, Dick spent most of the following year at Boccadon writing *Return From Utopia*, in which he urged a reduction in laws and regulations and a turning away from socialism. In this he had the support not only of many Conservatives but also of the Liberal Lord Rennell, who wrote: 'a particularly mischievous category of [wartime] orders arose out of a zeal for perfectionism, a desire by many Ministries and Civil Servants for everything, and especially everyone, to be tied up in bundles, to achieve uniformity.'

In March 1948 Sam and Kit's third daughter, Priscilla Jane, married John Bygott-Webb, who was a barrister by profession and had been a major in the army. The wedding reception was at the Hyde Park Hotel and Sam and Kit also gave an evening party for some hundred people. After leaving the Brighton College of Art, Priscilla had studied architecture at the AA but, as she was already married and pregnant with her first child when she got her degree, she did not join an architectural practice. However, later, when Sam bought Toll Farm, she designed a couple of cottages for him and she also did a conversion for him in London.

The war had made Kit enthusiastic about country life and the basic activities of growing food and rearing animals. In her 1948 diary she gives almost as much space to her chickens as she does to social engagements and a good deal more than she does to constituency appointments in East Willesden, where Sam was hoping to get in again at the next general election.

An entry for 6 April reads: 'sat hen on twelve eggs – two broke with their shells, four hatched, six left in cold by deadly, beastly hen.' Then two days later: 'put hen on thirteen eggs'. On the seventh she went to a Royal Empire Society lunch at Southend, where Dick was speaking. Then the Crumps came for the weekend and the following day she was in East Willesden and lunched with Mrs Hurst (Sam's agent), going in the evening to hear Churchill speak at the Albert Hall. Next was an entry: 'goose eggs down (28 days to hatch)', followed by Freddy Erroll's visit to Saxons and then 'with Keelings to a Point to Point'. She found a pheasant's nest in the herbaceous border with twelve eggs, which she took and put under a hen, giving the pheasant some chicken's eggs instead. The hen, however (was it the same deadly, beastly one?) failed to hatch out the pheasants but the pheasant did very well with the chickens and took them down to the woods, where they crowed loudly and roosted in the trees. In May, however, she had a success with another hen, the entry reading: 'fourth hen should be out', followed by: 'one infertile, one black, ten yellow. Hurrah!'

However, with Jenniver now a debutante, she had many social engagements. The school she had chosen for Jenniver was 'more noted for its careful instruction on social graces than for its academic rigour' (Patricia Bowes Lyon and Rayne McCorquodale were among her classmates). Kit notes in her diary that in June Jenniver and Sarah Macmillan went to a dance together, followed by the Macmillans' cocktail party on the twenty-sixth. The following week Sam and Kit took Jenniver to Glyndebourne with the Castle Stewarts and their youngest son, Simon (with whom Jenniver had been at nursery school). Rosamund Christie and Jenniver became friends and when the shock of her mother's death made Rosamund mentally ill, a condition from which she never totally recovered, Jenniver used to visit her in hospital and often had her to stay.

At the end of July Kit's diary shows that she stayed at Goodwood for three days for the races. After which, she records that Jenniver had to be in London for Gillian Beamish's dance and then back in Sussex for the Baxendales' party at Framfield Place. In August Kit and Sam went to Cornwall to stay with the Laws at Boccadon. Then an October entry reads: 'Willesden, Walm Lane' and 'lunch with Lallie' (Lowis). Later in October Kit lunched with Irene Noel-Baker and the day after with Mabel Parr (over from the Argentine and staying at Claridges). She notes that Jenniver went to Sarah (Macmillan)'s cocktail party and stayed out until four in the morning! Then there is an entry: 'Mary [Law] for the evening' followed the next day by: 'Dick back from America'. She lunched with her sister-in-law Gladys at the end of November and in December with Geoffrey Lowis. Other diary entries for December were for the Eridge Hunt Ball and Eleanor (Castle Stewart)'s dance.

In 1950 Jenniver married Michael White. The wedding took place in London with a host of attendants, among whom were several of Harold and Dorothy Macmillan's grandchildren (including Maurice's second son, Joshua, who died at the age of 19). Jenniver's portrait was on the first page of *Country Life* and a wedding photograph was in the *Tatler*. Michael's father was a rear admiral and the social occasion greatly pleased Kit. But Sam was saddened by the thought of yet another daughter leaving home. He was also saddened when a few months later his sister Constance's husband, John Snell, died from a heart attack aged only 56.

XIX

Directorships and Business Expansion

Sam continued to nurse East Willesden for the Conservatives but now that the war was over he had more time to concentrate on his various businesses. In the 1946 *Directory of Directors* he is listed as having the following directorships: Delta Mill (1919) Ltd, Devon Mill Ltd, Fernhurst Mill Ltd, Harbens (Viscose & Silk Manufacturers) Ltd, J. Mendleberg & Co. Ltd, Lily Mills Ltd, London & Coastal Oil Wharves Ltd, Rex Mill Ltd, Rugby Mill Ltd, S. Noton Ltd, Soudan Mill Co. Ltd, and Travel Goods Ltd.

This last company was in the Irish Republic, where the Orford family had been living since 1935 when they left Oldham. Sam was keen for S. Noton Ltd. to expand into Ireland and he had discussed the project with Henry Orford on a first investigative visit in 1940. Orford's name again appears in a diary entry in 1941. Now in 1945, following a meeting between himself, John Jervis, L.G. Polturak and Cyril Hammersley, he flew to Dublin to set up Travel Goods Ltd Portarlington. This was opened, with Orford as its manager, in 1949, S. Noton Ltd having a controlling stake in the company from which over the years it was to receive good dividends.

At S. Noton's main factory in Blackhorse Lane, Walthamstow, an ambitious expansion programme was started in anticipation of an increase in the demand for luggage now that (with certain monetary restrictions) people were again free to travel. L.G. Polturak (George) who was a graduate from Lwow Technical University, was appointed chief engineer and Sam bought a small subsidiary factory (the Roman Way Company) to make the metal locks and hinges, where he put George's older brother, Felix (who had been manager of the Polish airline LOT) in charge, with his son-in-law Bernard to train under him. Sam had wanted Bernard on the main board, but Bernard, whose heart had never been in anything but flying, did not feel either qualified or competent for such a position.

In Lancashire, Sam continued the process of rationalisation and consolidation that he had already begun. Cotton had made good profits in the war years when there was no foreign competition and the demand for cotton yarn exceeded the supply; but there were also many mills that had been mothballed. Over the next couple of years Sam worked on an amalgamation programme, originally proposing that the Delta, the Devon, the Fernhurst, the Lily and the Rugby should all be in one group. But he was opposed by his co-director William Noton, who thought this was too big a grouping, although he agreed to the amalgamation of the Soudan with the Rex to form Soudan Mill Holdings. However, by 1947 Sam had united the Delta, the Fernhurst and the Rugby to form Cotton & Rayon Spinners.

By the end of 1950, he was planning a business trip to Canada and America. Just before leaving, in March 1951, he made the following statement to the annual general meeting of Lily Mills Limited: 'As a country we cannot afford to obtain other than the utmost from our industrial equipment. The disparity of incomes between wage-earners in the US and wage-earners in other countries is due more to the greater application of science and technology than to greater natural resources.'

The objectives of his trip to North America were threefold: to obtain first-hand information on the production of synthetics on behalf of Harbens; to visit cotton mills to see the latest technical developments; and to make contacts in Canada for S. Noton Ltd. Harold Mandleberg, his co-director at Harbens, provided him with letters of introduction for the first objective. He also had letters of introduction to textile mills in both countries from C. Henniker-Heaton of the Federation of Master Cotton Spinners Association, who had headed a cotton spinning productivity team to New York the year before. In a letter to Barnes Textile Associates Inc. in Boston, Henniker-Heaton wrote: 'Mr Hammersley is not strictly a technical man himself but he is particularly concerned with bringing all those firms with which he is connected to the fore-front of technical progress and efficiency.' And in a further paragraph: 'if you are over in England at any time Mr Hammersley would be very pleased if you would visit one or more of his mills, as he would be glad to have your opinion as to how the steps being taken in them towards maximum productive efficiency match up with those being taken in progressive American firms.'

Sam wrote to Kit from Boston before going on to Alabama to see a (show) spinning mill, telling her: 'the textile business is very tough'. In Washington he got a ticket to listen to a debate in the Senate and in Montreal, where he negotiated a franchise for Noton suitcases, he heard a debate in the Canadian parliament.

On his return, he completed another amalgamation of mills. The Devon Mill, which he had recently modernised (qualifying it for a subsidy under the Cripps Plan) he united with the Lily, calling them Lily 1 and 2. He then incorporated both of them with Soudan Mill (Holdings). This became known as the Lily Mills Group and was now able to spin synthetic fibres as well as cotton. 'Share-holders may feel satisfied that we are by no means unmindful of the impact of new synthetic fibres on the textile industry', said Sam in his chairman's statement, in which he announced a dividend or 17.5 per cent.

Only a few months later, articles began to appear in the Lancashire press that the Lily Mills Group was to be sold. 'But to whom?' asked the journalists, unable to get Sam, who had been negotiating its sale over the past two

140

years, to reveal the name of the buyer, who wanted it kept secret. Then articles appeared in the national press with headlines such as: 'Big Cotton Bid Mystery' and 'A mystery man sent the shares of three Lancashire cotton mills soaring to more than four times their original price with a £1,150,000 offer to buy them'. Eventually it transpired that the bidder was Cyril Lord and the price he finally paid was £1,195,000.

Lord was a co-director of Sam's at Mandlebergs and a friend of William Noton. He was born in 1911, educated in Manchester and had been operating in the textile trade since 1945 as a merchant converter but he did not become a mill-owner until 1949, when he bought two small weaving mills. In a short time he had built up a textile empire and was soon making such outstanding profits that when in 1954, he went public and put the shares of the Lily Mills Group on the market, they were oversubscribed.

At Harbens, the word 'Rayon' (which had been a trade secret in the 1920s) replaced 'Viscose & Silk' in the company's title. Synthetic fibres were now all the rage but nylon was still very expensive. (Many women at this time, particularly refugees, managed to earn a living mending rayon and nylon stockings as they were far too highly prized to be thrown away as soon as they were laddered.) In 1948 Harbens celebrated its twenty-fifth anniversary with a party for all their workpeople at the Tower Ballroom, Blackpool, which was very much in the tradition of the Whitweek outings to Blackpool for cotton operatives. Seventy-eight coaches transported over 2,500 workers to and from Golborne for the occasion, where there was whist, dancing, a dinner and a mannequin parade of clothes and accessories made entirely of Harbens rayon yarn. (Traditionally, everyone wore new clothes for Whitweek.) The Chairman at Harbens was J. Harold Mandleberg, son of the founder, and L.C. Mandleberg was one of the other directors with Sam. Since 1937 Sam had also been a director of Mandlebergs, which made rainwear. The firm had done well in the war producing waterproof clothing for the forces but now, looking ahead to the ending of clothes rationing, they concentrated on the production of more fashion-conscious rainwear for the retail trade.

H. Moorcroft, who had joined London & Coastal Oil Wharves in 1937 and stayed with it until his retirement 21 years later, was made a director in 1946, joining Sam (who was Chairman) and Sylvester Gates. Moorcroft had seen the company through the difficult years of the war, when it was not allowed to store oil and had got no compensation. The storage facilities (170,000 tons on some 56 acres) were not, however, the only asset of LCOW, who had leased a total of 191 acres from the Port of London Authority, much of which was earmarked for industrial development. Together with Tecalemit, this was the most profitable of Forsyth & Partners' old assets.

When the date of the 1950 general election was announced, Sam and Kit moved up to their London flat in Chesham Street and on polling day Jenniver brought her pony and trap to East Willesden. There are photographs of her, looking very young and blonde, sitting in the trap, holding the reins, with Sam standing at the pony's head. It was taken outside the Conservative committee rooms at Walm Lane, Sam with the traditional huge rosette in the lapel of his impeccably tailored double-breasted dark suit and the pony-trap covered in electioneering posters. They must have attracted some attention but the picture they presented was not in tune with the aspirations of the electorate, only emphasising the difference in lifestyles between affluent country-dwellers and the deprived urban poor. Maurice Orbach, the sitting Labour member, got in again and Clement Attlee remained Prime Minister. The general public was, however, starting to have doubts about the advantages of socialism and this time Labour's majority was greatly reduced.

The new government was only just elected when, in June 1950, the Korean War broke out. There was widespread fear of it escalating and Attlee urged the necessity of an all-out, top-speed drive for armaments and other defence equipment. In 1946 *Picture Post* had featured a profile of Richard Stokes (no longer an MP) with the title 'Was There A Tank Scandal?' Now, with this new war, the *Evening News* called on Sam as 'the tank expert' and he wrote them a full-page article, printed with a box headline on the front page: 'Are We Building THE RIGHT TANKS?'

XX

Links With Israel

In East Willesden Jews made up a large and influential section of the electorate and as their MP Sam had taken an especial interest in them. He continued this interest for the rest of his life and when he died there were many tributes to him from influential Israelis and members of the Jewish community in Britain.

As early as 1917 the British had pledged support for a national home for the Jews in Palestine in a letter signed by Lord Balfour as Foreign Secretary to Lord Rothschild, President of the English Zionist Federation. (It was this letter that was afterwards called the Balfour Declaration.) Balfour had been won over to Zionism after meeting Chaim Weizmann in Manchester in 1906. Weizmann, who would become the first President of Israel, was a student at Manchester University and looked on England as his second home. As leader of the Zionists, he was, therefore, pleased that the British, at the end of the First World War, were given Palestine under the Mandate of the League of Nations. But the Balfour Declaration antagonised the Arabs, who were afraid of Jewish immigration and felt they should have been better rewarded for helping to defeat the Turks. But, even though Britain put a quota on the number of new Jewish immigrants they would let into Palestine, the Arabs were not appeased. The 1939 Government White Paper on Palestine, which set this quota at 75,000 over five years, was opposed by Sam who thought the number too low and he wrote a long article in the *Willesden Chronicle* to this effect, which was published with his picture.

His first speech to parliament after he was elected as member for East Willesden in 1938, was on the subject of Jewish refugees from Germany, supporting a motion proposed by Philip Noel-Baker. Great Britain and the Empire together, he said, were quite capable of absorbing the proposed figure of 500,000 Jews, and he cited the fact that one million Greeks were absorbed by Greece after the Turkish massacre in 1922. But he also advocated an immediate increase in the available immigration into Palestine which, he said, was ready and able to take some 50,000 extra immigrants. He also thought that Kenya and Tanganyika would benefit from an influx of 'intelligent and industrious individuals' and mentioned the Jewish capital available throughout the world, especially in the USA, that should be available to help them settle and which, he suggested, could be a possible trade-off for some of our American debt. This is a challenge, he said, which both practically and on humanitarian grounds Britain, the champion of the oppressed, cannot ignore. It was this speech that gave Sam the dubious honour of having his name reviled in a broadcast by Goebbels, the German Propaganda Minister.

Throughout the war he was a member of the Parliamentary Palestine Committee and asked several questions in the House about the formation of a Palestine regiment and about speeding up permits for Jews to enter Palestine. When there was a visit of British Council officials to the Middle East in 1942, the Jewish community was anxious and Sam asked the House for assurance that they had not gone on government business and that they were not involved in any secret agreements.

In October 1943, at the Parliamentary Palestine Committee dinner at the Dorchester, Sam introduced the chief speaker, Dr Weizmann. When Lord Wedgwood, who was Chairman of the Parliamentary Palestine Committee, died, Sam delivered a tribute to him to the Zionist Association and shortly afterwards succeeded him as Chairman. In December, his articles on honouring the

Balfour Declaration were in both the *Willesden Chronicle* and *The Times* and he spoke to Rotary Clubs in Manchester and Leeds on the subject of 'Post-war Palestine'. In January 1944 he had a letter published in *The Times* on the same subject, as well as in the *Jewish Chronicle*. In March he took part in the opening of Palestine House, which became the cultural centre for Jews until the formation of the State of Israel in 1948.

Immediately after the war, feelings ran high against the British Government's attempts to limit the number of Jews entering Palestine as newsreels featured boats overloaded with women and children who were not being allowed to land.

Sam's diary shows that during the autumn of 1949 he had meetings in Manchester both with the Midlands Pro-Palestine Committee and the Zionist Central Council. In November he gave a talk in London at the Anglo-Palestinian Club in Great Windmill Street on 'The British Cotton Industry & its links with the Textile Industry of Palestine'.

Although by 1950 Sam had lost East Willesden and was no longer an MP, far from losing interest in Jewish affairs, he formed strong ties with the newly established State of Israel and became the first Executive Chairman of the Anglo-Israel Association. Leo Amery and Robert Boothby were on the committee with him as was the actress Sybil Thorndike (Mrs Casson).

During 1951 he chaired three separate talks for the Anglo-Israel Association on subjects connected with the new state: 'Three Years in Israel', 'Israel Law in the Making' and 'New Situations in the Middle East'; the last was given by the Hon. Edwin Samuel, whose talk 'The Conquest of the Desert' Sam also chaired the following year. In 1952 he was in the chair again at a press conference for a British parliamentary delegation going to Israel and he and Kit hosted a reception for Israeli journalists.

Earlier that same year he was invited to be question master at a session of *The Brains Trust* to be held at Caxton Hall. The programme was broadcast each week by the BBC and covered a number of topical issues, Sam's being 'British Policy in the Middle East – Especially Israel'.

Speaking at the annual general meeting of the Anglo-Israel Association in 1953, Sam stated that the objective of the association was 'to explain and interpret Israel to Great Britain and to do the same in the reverse direction'. He appealed for more members, saying: 'this business of explaining and interpreting is the basis of all good friendly relations. In ignorance lies misunderstanding; in knowledge lies appreciation.'

In March he went to Israel with a group from the Anglo-Israel Association. He wrote to Kit from Lydda and again from Tel Aviv. He had, he reported, visited the Weizmanns in their home and Mrs Weizmann (Vera) sent her love to Kit. Chaim was not well. (He died the following year.) There was 'lots of talk everywhere'. He lunched with Sir Francis Evans, the British Minister, and had an appointment with Ben Gurion, the Israeli PM. On his return he wrote an enthusiastic article about the new state, its economic progress and the unifying role of its kibbutzim, which was published in the *Anglo-Israel Association Bulletin* with a photograph of the group, with Sam at its centre, in front of Solomon's Pillars.

In April 1953 he wrote a letter to *The Times* on the subject of Middle East defence and in September another of his letters on the Arab-Israeli situation, also published by *The Times*, gave rise to a long exchange of correspondence with, among others, the pro-Arab E.L. Spears. In his chairman's report to the Anglo-Israel Association in 1954, appealing for an increase in corporate membership, he said: 'I doubt if I am wrong in thinking that nine out of ten of the persons who have a voice in the moulding of public opinion in this country are ignorant of the problems of Israel and correspondingly unaware of how the tranquillity of the Middle East affects the economic health of Britain and the peace of the world. With the consent and approval of the United States,' he went on, 'Britain has made her peace with Egypt. There is, however, no under-

147

standing in this country that arms for Egypt's defence may mean arms for aggression against Israel'. In December 1955, a year before the Suez crisis, he spoke at a public meeting on a similar subject: 'Israel Faces Danger'.

Sam was Chairman of the Anglo-Israel Association's Grants Committee during 1958 and 1959 and he was also a member of the Finance Committee from then until 1962, when, trying to reduce his workload, he resigned. He made investments via his stockbroker, Anthony Sancroft-Baker, on behalf of the Windham Deedes Memorial Fund, of which he was a trustee; he sponsored one of the association's travel scholarships, Mr S.S. Hammersley's Award, and it was thanks to him that Harbens and J. Mandleberg & Co, as well as S. Noton Ltd, became covenanted and corporate subscribers to the Anglo-Israel Association. He invited influential political friends to the fund-raising concerts and dinners organised by the association and many of them spoke at the public meetings which he chaired.

When Eliahu Elath became Israeli Ambassador to London in 1957, he invited Sam to meet the Knesset delegation to the Inter-Parliamentary Conference, and in 1958 Sam went to Israel as an official member of the delegation to take part in the ceremonies in the Balfour Forest at which a memorial was unveiled to Lord Balfour's niece and biographer, Blanche Dugdale. A photograph shows him on the platform with Ben Gurion, the Prime Minister, with among others Lady Violet Bonham Carter and Mrs Vera Weizmann (Chaim's widow). After the speeches all the VIPs, including Sam, planted trees. In 1959 he became a member of the Royal Institute of International Affairs.

XXI

Fighting for a Friend

Sam missed the House of Commons but he decided not to stand again although there was another election the year after he lost East Willesden, in which Churchill came back as Prime Minister (at the age of 85!) with Macmillan in his Cabinet. However, he still kept in touch with his many political friends, meeting them in the House and in his clubs, and when the new Commons chamber was opened he was invited to the ceremony. He also encouraged the next generation trying to get into parliament, writing a supporting letter for Oliver Stutchbury when he stood as the Conservative candidate in East Rhondda in 1951. (Later Oliver joined the Labour Party and then formed a party of his own to abolish the GLC.)

He still discussed monetary policy with Norman Crump, who was now Financial Editor on the *Sunday Times*, and he had not given up his belief that a once-only capital levy should be imposed on war profits. In 1949 he wrote a letter to the Chancellor of the Exchequer, thinking that a Labour government might look favourably on the idea. But no reply is among his papers and it would seem that socialists were as loath as were Conservatives to grasp such a prickly nettle.

When Robert Boothby was created a life peer, Sam wrote to congratulate him and among his papers there is a letter written to 'Dear Sam' in which Boothby writes: 'This makes a good ending to a long political stint and I shall be glad to shed the growing burdens and stresses of life in the House of Commons and yet remain a Member of

149

Parliament.' There is also another handwritten note from him, signed 'Bob', replying to a letter Sam had written to him the previous August when he (Boothby) was in the King Edward VII Hospital.

Dick Law was now Lord Coleraine and also sat in the House of Lords. He and Mary continued to spend weekends at Saxon Court and the two couples also met regularly in London during the week. Dick became Chairman of Atomic Power and also a director of Horlicks, promoting a new beverage made from whey, which, in spite of Mary's loyal praise of it, neither Sam nor Kit found drinkable.

In 1955 Frederick Erroll, after he returned from visiting Russia with a parliamentary delegation, invited Sam to the viewing of a Soviet film of the occasion and later lunched with him at Brooks's. Sam took the prevalent British view of the Soviet threat: 'it couldn't happen here' and he tried to calm the fears of his Polish son-in-law, Bernard. But Bernard had first-hand information concerning the aggressive intentions of the Russians. His sister's stepson had visited him and urged him to return to Poland so as to be 'on the winning side'. At this time only trusted members of the Communist Party were allowed out of Poland (or Russia).

Harvey Combe was the friend Sam had been fighting for ever since the end of the war. Harvey was faced with huge income tax demands which he did not feel were just and which he could not pay. Sam had put him in touch with a good Manchester lawyer and written letters in support of his claims on the Ministry of Supply. They lunched together several times in 1945, both at Brooks's and at the Savoy Grill. In 1946 Harvey's passport shows that he went to Sweden, probably to get support from the Bofors people there, and in 1948 he went more than once to Brussels. Eventually, according to a note in Sam's handwriting, he was able to have the original demand, which was for £260,000, reduced to £30,000. Nevertheless, in March 1949 Harvey was declared a bankrupt.

150

Harvey had government contracts dating back to before the war for the delivery to Britain of Bofors guns from Sweden. But Sweden was neutral. In 1940 and 1941, when Britain stood alone against Germany, these guns were urgently needed and Harvey entered into an agreement with the British Government to enable them to be manufactured in the United States under the licence that he held from Bofors. His passport shows that he made several trips to the United States during those years, sometimes through Portugal (which was neutral) and sometimes via Bermuda. This would only have been possible with special government permission. However, when Lend-Lease came into operation, the British Government withdrew from the transaction and Harvey was left with his commissions unpaid.

Sam had lent him money before the war, which should have been repaid in 1940. But it was only when he was declared a bankrupt that Sam presented the receivers in bankruptcy with evidence of it. 'The money was advanced', he wrote, 'against orders placed by the British Government with Messrs. Bofors. I held the list of contracts and expected deliveries, which was given to me as some kind of collateral security. It will be appreciated that when the war broke out the delivery of a lot of these contracts was frustrated by enemy action.'

The Inland Revenue, however, backed by the Treasury, still would not relent. To try and break the deadlock, Sam turned to Frederick Erroll, who, now Conservative MP for Altrincham & Sale, offered to do what he could to get the matter reviewed. The case against the Ministry of Supply, he wrote, was basically that 'Captain Combe's natural expectations of commission were frustrated by the invention of a form of inter-governmental assistance – namely Lend Lease – which was hitherto unknown in either commercial or international law' and further that 'Captain Combe was not so informed until many years after the event'.

A huge correspondence arguing this case went back and

forth between Sam, Freddy, the solicitors and Henry Brooke at the Treasury. The Inland Revenue eventually agreed to give Harvey a temporary allowance of £3 a week. But the Treasury argued: 'his debts to the Revenue arise from assessments on actual profits which he made', adding 'we have gone to the limit of generosity'. Even when in the spring of 1955 Freddy became Parliamentary Secretary at the Ministry of Supply, he could not get the authorities to change their minds.

Oaklands, the Combes' house at Sedlescombe, had been compulsorily sold and, together with the outbuildings, had become a Pestalozzi village. His wife Terry was living with her stepdaughter in a basement in Bayswater. Harvey, who was partially blind, was living in a nursing home in St Leonards. Sam visited him there several times but in June 1955 had to write saying: 'I am rendered very immobile with an acute attack of rheumatism. Hope to come and see you next week.' But by July Harvey was in a serious state of bad health and had to go into hospital and Sam was himself in a nursing home.

He wrote to Henry Brooke asking for the Treasury to release £100 to cover Harvey's 'hospital expenses', which they agreed to do, with the proviso that, when he was better, even the £3 a week allowance would be stopped. Terry was suffering from arthritis but she managed to scribble a letter to Sam to tell him that Harvey was on a drip, waiting for an operation on his heart. He died on 10 August 1955.

Sam was greatly saddened, particularly as he had not been able to go and see Harvey at the end. The first thing he did when he came out of the nursing home at 35 Weymouth Street was to make sure that the Treasury released sufficient funds to pay not only for Harvey's 'hospital expenses', as agreed, but also his nursing home bill and his cremation expenses.

Apart from the trusts Sam had set up for members of his family, he had a couple of other trusteeships. One was for Mrs Bray (the mother of Dr John Bray, who used to stay at Littlestone), which he had run since 1945 with the help of his accountant, Percy Westhead. The bulk of this trust she left on her death in 1951 to her son and two daughters but she also left £43,000 in trust for her grandchildren. John Bray became interested in the problems of old age and a prime mover in the founding of geriatrics as a branch of medicine. He wrote to Sam for support and Sam gave a seven-year covenant, through CARS, to the London Postgraduate Medical School for this purpose and got Dick Coleraine to do the same, through Horlicks.

Sam's second trusteeship was with The Hon. Vera Bingham, for Earl Castle Stewart's two surviving sons, Patrick and Simon. He was also an East Sussex Commissioner, trying tax disputes and appeals in the county's three divisions: Crawley, Tunbridge Wells and Uckfield, and in 1951 he was elected an underwriting member at Lloyd's.

Philip Howard interviewed him for *The Times* and wrote a not-very-flattering sketch, which Kit took exception to, in which he referred to his 'earnest, pale blue eyes'. Philip Howard himself turned out later to be the more earnest of the two as he joined Moral Re-Armament. Sam never did, although his old friends from the First World War, Queenie and Leo Exton, tried to recruit him. They and all their family were committed to Moral Re-Armament and worked for it, first from its headquarters in Hays Mews and later from 117 Eaton Square, where they kept open house. 'Sam and Kitty' were often invited there, as well as to the plays that the movement put on at the Westminster Theatre. Leo presented Moral Re-Armament to Sam as 'a practical political solution in the fight against Communism'. The Soviets were estimated to be spending some £70 million a year on broadcasts to Asia, Africa and the Middle East, and the movement held conferences at Caux on 'Democracy v Communism'.

In August 1958 Leo wrote to Sam: 'I have been thinking over our conversation of last evening and wondering if I had heard you correctly when I thought you said that you would not presume to think that you could do anything towards bringing a change in world conditions.' He upbraids him for lack of faith, concluding the letter by saying: 'with God's help, ordinary men and women, many less significant than you, are proving the value of moral standards.' He also elicited practical help from Sam, writing to ask if he could provide cheap, strong suitcases at a discount for Moral Re-Armament workers going all over the world.

XXII

More Business

In 1954 the *Manchester Guardian* reported that the financial results of Cotton & Rayon Spinners were 'far above average'. When Sam made his Annual Chairman's Report to his various companies there was often a political element in them and in 1956 he sent his report to Cotton & Rayon Spinners to Frederick Erroll, who was Parliamentary Secretary to the Board of Trade. Freddy wrote back saying: 'I am passing it [your report] down to the appropriate section in the Board of Trade as I think it would do them good to have a look at it.'

Sam's report said:

Uncertainty and lack of confidence in the future continue to be the main bug-bears of the Lancashire cotton industry. Uncertainty has arisen because it has been anyone's guess as to how the surplus American cotton crop is to be marketed; lack of confidence because the trade is obviously vulnerable to unlimited imports of cloth and yarn produced in countries with large reservoirs of inexpensive labour. Moreover, the structure of the industry is not one which is well adapted to meet the foreign competition of today; there are too many sources from which orders can originate. This leads to short runs and uneconomic production. There is insufficient linkage between various sections of the industry. This means that available economies do not reach the consumer.

Sam advocated a combination of vertical and horizontal links, which he described as pisciform organisation with a large number of fins represented by the horizonal sections of the industry and a small number of backbones represented by the vertical combines. The point is, he explained 'that the fins and the backbone should articulate in conformity.' He acknowledged, however, that 'such modification of structure, however desirable, could not be brought about by mere discussion, that some practical incentives were necessary' and he suggested that the Yarn Spinners Association might well be the organisation to study the practical means by which sectional trade links could be encouraged.

'There is more to be done within the industry itself', he continued, 'before our burdens can be thrust in the lap of the Government. It is an illusion to suppose that healthy trading conditions can be maintained irrespective of the contributions made by the trade itself and, speaking of the trade itself, I am not unaware that probably the most powerful voice therein is that of organised labour.'

He then spoke of the large sums of money ploughed back into Cotton & Rayon Spinners since 1950 in the form of fixed stock:

This modernisation expenditure is a substantial contribution towards the maintenance of employment in the future. In a sense, shareholders' present sacrifices form a contribution towards the permanence of future wages. Yet this view of the part played by capital in the maintenance of employment is in conflict with the view that capital takes too much and wages too little from our economic system. It is in even sharper conflict with the view of at least one Trade Union secretary that 'it is up to every employee to get the maximum amount of wages for the least quantity of work his employer is prepared to accept.' The reason that new machinery in America is more productive

156

than here is that there all concerned believe it their duty to support new inventions to the utmost. If we cling to old methods and old standards the industry will inevitably decline. In such a declension it may be that those who are now in a position to give the greatest help – organised labour – will suffer most.

In 1958 Sam resigned from Harbens and both he and Cyril Lord resigned from Mandlebergs. Cyril came to dinner with Sam at 19 Chesham Street wearing a dinner jacket with a full-length, pale pink tie and tennis shoes (he was a keen tennis player). Having floated the Lily Mill so successfully, he now had offices in Cavendish Square and was already preparing to launch his tufted-rayon carpet business. He was also buying mills in Northern Ireland and planned to open another office in Belfast. When the business was launched he advertised with such slogans as 'Sensational carpet – sensational price!' and sold directly from the factories in Lancashire and Northern Ireland, opening his own retail shops in prime sites such as Marble Arch. The carpet group shot up from 1.6 million in 1958 to 5.9 million in 1960. Its sensational collapse, which bankrupted Cyril, did not occur until 1968 (after Sam's death).

Sam's luggage business, S. Noton Ltd, was also expanding, but more cautiously. In 1953 (coronation year) the 'crown' logo was adopted and with it the trade name Crown Luggage. The crown was made from the word 'Noton' by exaggerating the central 'T' and leaving the 'no' and 'on' on either side of it in lower case, the whole underlined with a thick curved line. By this time, with the accent already on air travel, the firm was producing a wide range of light suitcases in matching sets as well as hard-fibre, paxall-expanding and soft-topped. It also made document cases, weekend and attaché cases, fitted vanity cases, trunks and wooden tuck boxes, as well as industrial containers, and had agents in 32 countries. The terylene suitcase linings were made by Cotton &

Rayon Spinners at the Fernhurst Mill and the metal fittings continued to be designed and made at Roman Way.

In 1956 Sam bought Parker Wakeling, a firm making Victor luggage, leathergoods and handbags, and made it a wholly-owned subsidiary of S. Noton Ltd, with his son-in-law, Michael White, in charge. At the Leathergoods Fair in February 1957, the Victor Viceroy, a moulded suitcase of cellulose fibreglass, was launched. There was an article in the *Evening Standard* about it under the title 'Here's Something In The Bag'. 'Britain is doing well in new ideas', it read; 'the cases are lighter and stronger than the ordinary kind. A small car has been driven over one of these Noton's new products without making a dent.' Notons, the article said, had big orders from the fair and were doubling production space to meet demand. 'Head of the Noton firm is Mr Samuel Hammersley. He should know quite a bit about tough materials. He was in tanks in both world wars. His firm has paid good dividends for many years. Last time the shareholders had 15%'.

Although Victor lines were made by Parker Wakeling at Tottenham, the research and engineering for this new luggage, 'Europe's first moulded suitcase', was done by L.G. Polturak at the main Notons factory in Walthamstow. Here Sam, as always keen to take advantage of the latest technology, embarked on a big reorganisation programme, dividing the home market from exports and wholesale. He put Felix Polturak (who was now a director) in charge of computerising the whole factory, buying large and delicate machines (the only ones available at this time) that required to be housed in a special room, access to which was through a dust-proof curtain. By January 1955 Notons were making record profits and there was a scrip issue of shares. The Port-arlington factory in Ireland reported a 20 per cent return on investment and the catalogue boasted that S. Noton Ltd was 'the world's largest manufacturers of luggage and handbags'.

In February 1953 an article appeared in the *Stock*

Exchange Gazette about London & Coastal Oil Wharves which was sufficiently facetious to have been written by Sam himself. 'Questions at the meeting of London & Coastal Oil Wharves on Tuesday', it read, 'brought forth one or two interesting items of information: (inter alia) a shareholder and customer complimented the managing director, Mr H. Moorcroft, on the efficiency of his organisation but suggested the desirability of appointing an equally efficient deputy to carry on when he might be absent. This suggestion brought forth a rather significant reply from the chairman, Mr S.S. Hammersley: "We regard our company as a grown-up daughter, but we are not quite certain whether she should be groomed for a career or for marriage." The point is', the article went on, 'that the young lady dwells on a site of 192 acres in the mouth of the Thames and her neighbours are giants of the oil industry. The nearest of these, though not the biggest, is Trinidad Leaseholds. The idea seems to be that she will continue her career of single blessedness until the big oilman embraces her.'

Sam had several meetings at Yugoslav House during the war on behalf of Forsyth & Partners and met King Peter at Claridges, later attending a Yugoslav reception. He held debentures with a face value of £500 in Podrinje Consolidated Mines, which he (for the directors) and P.R. Scutt (as secretary) had issued in 1945, following Eddy Forsyth's optimistic letter of October 1944 saying he was hoping to get the money back 'now that Belgrade is free'. But, with the Communists in power, Belgrade was far from free and the best that could be managed was a small distribution spread over four years, and by 1959 an official receiver and liquidator was appointed by the High Court. P.R. Scutt became Managing Director of Tecalemit Ltd, which had also been in Forsyth & Partners, and in which Sam was a shareholder.

In 1956 Sir Irving Albery, whom Sam had known since they were in the House of Commons together, asked him to draw up a scheme for turning the Albery family theatres into a public company. This Sam did, advocating the buying from the trustees of the head leases of the New Theatre and of Wyndhams Theatre and the issue of some 50,000 new shares at a premium. In the autumn of 1957 he was asked to join the Wyndhams Theatres Board.

When Wyndhams Theatres Ltd acquired the Criterion Theatre in 1959 new lighting was required and Sam, who had been shown the stage-lighting system at Glyndebourne by John Christie when it was new, wrote to him asking if he might suggest that Donald Albery get in touch with him. There were four members of the Albery family on the board and Sam remained a director until his death. He advised the company on investments and in 1958, when Anglia TV was in its infancy, suggested that it should take up the shares. Nothing, however, came of this. His was a financial role and he kept a close eye on the accounts. When congratulated on the success of *The Miracle Worker* (about a deaf and dumb girl who was taught to speak), which was playing to packed houses, he said: 'Yes, but the bar takings are down; those audiences don't drink!' The list of plays that the company put on between 1958 and 1965 included *Oliver*, *Chin-Chin*, *Dear Liar*, *The Rose Tattoo*, *Sparrers Can't Sing* and *A Taste of Honey*. Sam went to most of the first nights.

XXIII

Family Affairs

In 1954 the tenant who farmed at Toll Farm, the land immediately adjacent to Saxon Court, died, and when it came on the market Kit persuaded Sam to buy it. He was not himself attracted to farming but, characteristically, once he had it he wanted to make a success of it, investing heavily in improvements to the buildings and to the stock. Grappling with milk yields and subsidies, he wrote to Dick Coleraine at his farm, Bocaddon, asking his advice about a lactometer and saying: 'I am most anxious to get first class results from my herd'. He also sought help from Michael McFall, who farmed at Piltdown and was a farm manager by profession. Michael was courting his youngest daughter, Philippa, and was often over at Saxon Court.

Philippa had spent six months in Paris at the Sorbonne and now, in 1955, she was doing 'the season' and being presented at court. In June Sam and Kit gave a dance for her at the Grosvenor House Hotel, during which she was photographed for the *Tatler*, sitting on a sofa with her four sisters. Dick Coleraine teased Sam that he was more nervous about this dance than about making a speech in the House of Commons. It was also nervous-making for Philippa, particularly as Kit would not allow her to wear her glasses although she was very short-sighted.

In 1956 Sam's sister Gladys died after a short illness, and in the autumn of that same year Philippa and Michael McFall were married. As they lived so close, Michael was able to allocate several hours a week to Toll Farm. However, by 1957 it was making losses of between three and four thousand pounds a year and, in spite of an entry in Sam's diary: 'sold a bull for 180 guineas', he also wrote: 'farm a bad business'.

After Philippa married, Nanny left Saxons and went to live in Wiltshire with two of her sisters. Sam gave her a small retirement pension and she kept in touch with all the girls, remembering their birthdays, and writing to Kit from time to time. Sam gave each of his daughters a settlement when they were married, tying up the capital for the benefit of their children. Kit was particularly keen for this to be done in case the husbands should leave them. These trusts were similar to the ones he had set up for his sisters when their father died and he administered them himself with the help of his accountant, Percy Westhead. He also made covenants for all his grandchildren, of which there were 16 by the time he died.

Kit had always resisted Sam's efforts to teach her to keep accounts. She was regularly overdrawn and in the days when tradesmen sent in books, she was always late in paying them. Every month his efforts to reform her ended in an ugly row. Now he had given up and paid everything himself, giving her a small monthly allowance for her own needs. These were not excessive as she lived frugally and, although she had good taste in clothes, she did not set much store by them. She collected fine china but, although she and Mary Coleraine often went to auctions together, she rarely bid without Sam. Her idea of relative costs was so hazy that her grandchildren joked that at one moment she would say: 'don't take too much sugar', and in the next breath ask them if they would like an aeroplane.

Sam dismissed her practical shortcomings as typical of women. But he consulted her, respected her opinions, and often found her insights about people helpful. She was sympathetic to personal problems and during 1955 became involved with the Noel-Bakers' two little grandsons, who had been deserted by their mother, and had them to stay for the summer at Saxon Court. Both boys were born at

Achmetaga in Greece but had been brought back to England for Edward to see medical specialists. Francis, their father, was now Labour MP for Swindon.

In February 1956 their grandmother Irene died. It is a measure of Kit's involvement that she went with the Coleraines to the interment; normally she let Sam attend such occasions on his own. (There were also memorial services for Irene in St Martin's-in-the-Fields and St Paul's church, Athens.)' Philip, who in 1959 was awarded the Nobel Peace Prize, asked Kit what she thought would be the best thing to do for the two boys and, writing to her in March, said: 'Thank you for seeing Francis and me and for your very wise advice. Francis has now agreed that we shall go out together with Edward to Greece on Monday next by train.'

But the children's mother, Anne, felt that her rights were being ignored and in March of the following year, Philip turned to 'Dearest Kit' again. 'This is the third case in nine months that Anne has brought', he wrote. 'In the first two she did not suggest access to the children; she only wanted to prevent Francis taking them abroad'. He sent Kit copies of his affidavit, which he hoped she would support. Edward, who had suffered from various illnesses since babyhood, was mentally unstable and needed a safe home. His grandfather was fearful of the dangers of another change of surroundings, especially as now Francis planned to marry again. He was, however, confident that the new wife would be 'much kinder and more dependable than Anne ever was'.

Thinking that an outside interest would be good for Kit and knowing how indignant she always was about neglected children, Sam encouraged her to do some social work in the form of school visiting in Homerton. But she soon discovered that her judgemental approach to their parents, which might have been acceptable when she did similar work in Battersea in the 1920s, was now resented, so that her intervention only made matters worse. Unable to face the ugly scenes, she lost herself in the tenement blocks and did not keep her appointments. Sam had to go to the school, make excuses and hand in her resignation.

To cheer her up after this failure, he arranged for her to have a holiday in Paris and, although she never liked travelling and particularly hated the Channel crossing, she went to stay with Marion (now divorced from Claude and married to Paul Arnoux). Sam wrote her a sarcastic letter:

> I hear that you arrived safely after a good crossing. How miserable for you! I think of you bearing the almost insufferable burden of Paris in June with the possibility of having to spend a week-end exploring the gracious chateaux of the Loire. There will be blue skies, green leaves, twittering persons on the boulevards, entrancing shops, good food ... my heart bleeds for you! Here all is gaiety: the bewitching stimulation of a London Coastal meeting is succeeded the following day by the unforgettable panache of a meeting at Notons. So one day of delirious delight follows another. Today I had lunch with Cyril Lord. However, you must be brave and not return to these delights too soon.

Three days later he wrote again, after receiving a 'charming though almost illegible postcard'. This time, although the letter starts amusingly enough, it ends on a more serious note. Kit, he gathered from the postcard, intended to bring Marion's cook back with her to England. 'I wonder if it would work', Sam wrote. 'You would have to reconcile yourself to a much higher standard of wastefulness and a much lower standard of efficiency than you allow yourself'. He knew, however, that it was not very likely that this Frenchwoman would be able to satisfy Kit's increasingly capricious and unrealistic expectations any more than had the many married couples he had recently engaged for her for Saxon Court. He finished the letter hoping she was enjoying herself and having a complete break so that she would 'return mentally and physically refreshed'.

He idealised her. Everything he did he laid, as it were, at her feet. When he was in Sweden on business in March 1954, he wrote to her:

How can an elderly married man write a love letter to his well beloved – I mean his wife? Clearly he cannot say anything new because, ex hypothesis, that would reveal a facet of his character of which she is unaware and he knows quite well that there is no facet of his character, or anything else that is his, of which she is not fully cognisant. He cannot say 'I love you' because she has heard him say that before on quite a lot of occasions and whatever it may mean in the glow of proximity it must mean less in the diffuseness of distance. How then can the problem be solved? But isn't the poor old man, the sweet old fathead, creating a problem where none exists? The problem he thinks the years have created, the years have in fact solved. Therefore I write no love letter but subscribe the best love letter I know – devotedly, Bundy.

He wrote from Manchester: 'Don't worry about the servants they are not worth it. Rest, my darling; I want you to look beautiful'. However, all the love was not on his side. In the July 1955 copy of *Country Life* she marked a poem for him with the word 'darling': 'Tired of life?' Not I!' With my true love standing by.' Yet, there were signs that his devotion irked her and when they argued, unable to get the better of him, she complained of his cold logic. He wrote to her from London in December (on old House of Commons notepaper): 'I will *try* to behave better in future. This is a humble and abject apology.' He does not say exactly what he had done, or not done, but goes on: 'will you in turn restore to me those little intimacies on which our lives in the past were based. I mean the occasional revealing smile, the touches when we meet, the unpremeditated embrace. I feel when I am

165

talking to you that I am talking to a stranger, and a highly critical one at that. Devotedly, Bundy.'

But he did not lose his sense of humour and, in spite of the considerable increase in the size of those double chins that she used to tease him about, he worked in his beloved rockery in the garden at Saxon Court, humming the song *Home on the Range*, with its line 'where seldom is heard a discouraging word', and thinking of new ways in which he could please her.

In February 1955, he wanted her to go to the South of France with him, her brother Jeff and Mary Coleraine's sister Martha Nellis; but she refused. In a letter he sent her from Nice he enclosed a small painting, on the back of which he wrote: 'Of course I didn't do it!' I left my paint box at home!' However, in April 1957 when he planned another holiday with Jeff, this time to Spain, she consented to go with them. Jeff organised the trip with the help of his stepson (Eve's son from her first marriage), who lived in Madrid with his English wife. They made all the arrangements, getting the airline tickets, booking hotels and hiring cars, so that for Sam it was an unusually relaxing and pleasant trip which he greatly enjoyed. On his return he wrote a long letter of thanks, enclosing his cheque for the last outstanding expenses.

However, Kit's suspicions of her brother Jeff had somehow been aroused. Under their uncle Bernard's will he was appointed trustee of the Netherton Farm Estate, and their uncle Tom, who was a solicitor, trustee of the Hutton Estates (both in Birmingham). Uncle Bernard had bequeathed Kit a house in Guernsey, for life, which she received in 1938, before the death of his widow, who had married again. Kit inherited the tenant together with the house, which was insured by Wakley & Wakley of Birmingham for a premium of £1 10s a year. She guarded the rent-book jealously and did not want Sam to interfere. He did not, therefore, ask to see the will of Bernard's unmarried sister Nell when she died in 1942, leaving her share of the family's property in Birmingham

166

entailed to Kit. When he referred to it, Jeff and Kit both assured him that the property could not be split up as long as the last of the older generation, their uncle Tom, was still alive. Tom died in 1951 and at this time Jeff took over the responsibility of insuring Kit's house in Guernsey (which was entailed to his son Peter).

Kit had always spoken of one of the Wakley properties her grandmother had bought in Birmingham as 'the donkey's field'. A share in this was what she believed her aunt Nell had left her in her will. But nearly ten years later she had still not received any information about it, although she suspected that Jeff had already sold it to Dunlop, who were to build a new factory on the site.

Sam sent a letter to Jeff, which stated: 'In connection with the proposed sale of property at West Bromwich and Aston, Birmingham, I think it is my duty in Kit's interest to make some formal enquiries.' Although he had copies of uncle Bernard's English and Guernsey wills, he had never seen either Nell's will or Tom's. When he did, he noticed that Tom had drawn up a new will not long before the date of his death, the legal wording of which left everything to Jeff's discretion, in spite of the clear intention of Nell's earlier will that her share should go to Kit.

Sam wrote another letter to Jeff in November 1961 in which he set out what he considered to be Jeff's moral obligation to his sister. The letter was not very diplomatic and Jeff in his short reply stated that of course he would look after her but he did not consider himself under any legal obligation. To this, within the week, Sam wrote another, longer letter, in which he wrote of his satisfaction at having set up settlements for his sisters after his father's death, although everything was legally his. Jeff did not reply. He made all the property over to his son Peter, who sold the Aston Cross properties in Lichfield Road and Park Road to Tube Investments. So much for keeping the Wakley properties intact!' No share of the money raised by these sales, nor from the sale of Cheniston Gardens, the Wakley house in Kensington, which Jeff (or Peter) also

167

sold, came to Kit. It was at this time that Peter (and his wife) joined the Scientologists.

Sam did not néed the Wakley money but it was important, psychologically, for Kit. His solicitors, Theodore Goddard, agreed that the circumstances of Tom's will were suspicious and they undertook to try and trace a Miss Elsie Isobel Smith, formerly of Aston Cross, Birmingham, who was Tom's housekeeper at Cheniston Gardens at the time of his death. She had witnessed the will and received a small legacy.

The enquiry agents employed by the solicitors could not find Elsie Smith. However, they did send in a report from a Mr Mould, who had a tobacconist's and newsagent's shop under the offices of Wakley & Wakley in Aston Cross, Birmingham. This gave an amusing account of Tom.

Mr Thomas Finsbury Wakley was a funny old man. He was so eccentric that he could not go into some of the properties he leased as the lessees would have thrown him out in the road. I have known him come to the office from London and burn a candle to save electricity. He would go over to the Co-op and buy half a loaf for his food. This was the latter days of course, although he was always hard as a nut and mean! He was definitely a bit mental towards the end, really eccentric – you know what I mean – like senile.

The verdict of senility seemed to be confirmed by the post-mortem on Tom which had been ordered by the coroner. 'The cause of death', it read, 'was myocardial fibrosis due to atheroma.'

'This', the solicitor's letter suggested, 'may well have a prejudicial effect on the mental capacity of the sufferer.'

XXIV

Feeling His Age

Sam and Kit now left their flat in Chesham Street and bought a little, unconverted mews flat over two garages. They were obliged by council regulations to keep one pair of big garage doors but, with her interior-decorating skills, Kit managed to use the space behind them as a dining room with a connecting kitchen. The garage on the other side of the front door became the living room, with a wide window. From the old chauffeur's flat upstairs, she made two connecting bedrooms, for herself and Sam, with a bathroom between; a housekeeper's room, another bathroom and a workroom for Sam's secretary. She enjoyed the planning and the decorating of it and made a garden area by putting troughs of flowers outside on the cobbled mews.

It was here that in 1962 Killi da Pauli painted her portrait. Like all the portraits of her, and there were five, it failed to catch anything of her spontaneous charm, making her look cold and haughty. But she liked it and a couple of years later she asked the same artist to do one of Sam. Because da Pauli wanted to please Kit and she kept drawing his attention to Sam's elegant hands, he painted them excessively long and narrow. He also gave him a long, narrow face and a disdainful expression. The portrait showed nothing of Sam's 'bluntness, his shrewdness and his utter lack of pomposity' which Lord Coleraine was to write of in his obituary of him, and above all nothing of 'his gaiety, by which', he said, 'he would best be remembered by all his friends'.

Already at Saxon Court Sam was trying to cut down on his commitments. He no longer ran the market garden, which letters to Percy Westhead show had always made losses, but he liked to work in the garden, particularly in the rockery, and every winter pored over seed catalogues, discussing with Kit what she would like him to order in the way of flowers and vegetables, so that he could plan the next season with the gardener. He also liked to put a bit of money on the horses every week and had an account with a firm called Scotland, who sent him packs of cards at Christmas with their thistle logo.

His chief outdoor recreation, apart from gardening, was now shooting. He was a member of a local shooting syndicate run by his friend and neighbour John Baxendale, and from 1958 until his death went shooting most weekends, often with his son-in-law, Michael White. There was an incident in which, shooting a bit too close to the road, a young woman with a child in a pushchair was sprayed with shot. She was not seriously hurt and the offending 'gun', when taken to court, was only given a caution. Sam could not resist making a bit of a joke about 'the peppered nursemaid' and the spot was thereafter known as 'nursemaid's corner'.

His friend John Stourton also enjoyed his weekend shooting. He wrote to 'My dear Sambo' in 1958, saying: 'It is the best game season for some years and I have enjoyed some nice days partridge driving.' John regretted that he could not dine with Sam on the suggested date (they had seen each other the previous week at the Carlton Club) because he would be shooting in East Anglia.

In 1960 Sam and Kit went on a Hellenic cruise on the *Ankara* for which the guide was Sir Mortimer Wheeler, joining the ship in Venice, where they stayed at the Hotel Cipriani. This was the last time that Kit went abroad with Sam. The following winter he went with Dick Coleraine to Tenerife and in January 1963, when he wanted to go to Egypt, as Kit said she preferred her own comfortable bed to staying in hotels, he took his daughter Priscilla. He

170

needed to get out of England in the winter for his health. His chesty colds were getting worse as he got older and they lasted longer and he was already looking to lighten his workload and to take life more easily.

Ironically, while Sam was trying to do less, Arthur Castle Stewart felt that he was not doing enough and was oppressed by feelings of uselessness. There had never been any economic pressure on him to work because of his wife's fortune and, although he had been an MP for a short time in the 1930s, he had no particular interests. He had recently been in two different nursing homes and his doctors had given him a collar to relieve the acute 'arthritic' stiffness in his neck; but he was still in pain.

Sam was worried about him. He believed that the loss of his two elder sons, David, killed at the Anzio landings, and Robert, who died of his wounds later in the Italian campaign, was preying on his mind. He knew that he was proud of them because he sent him a copy of the letter that David's CO had written praising him. But all four of the boys had been in America at the outbreak of war, staying on the Guggenheim ranch, and could have remained there had not both Arthur and Eleanor believed that it was their duty to return.

All his life Arthur, who was fond of quoting Kipling's 'If', had kept a stiff upper lip (he had been a schoolmaster before he inherited the title). However, when Sam spoke to him, he unexpectedly opened his heart, saying that over the years he had come to feel that his importance to his wife had so decreased that she no longer cared if he was dead or alive. He had come to see her great friend Vera Bingham as an obstacle between them, barring him access to Eleanor, and felt marginalised and unwanted. For years the two women had been going away on holiday together and now, as they got older, they were spending more and more time together, so that it seemed to him that Vera was always at his house.

Sam did not feel that he could speak to Eleanor but he planned to speak to Vera, who, although both women were

171

fond of him, he felt to be more approachable. Vera probably did not know how Arther felt. However, the more he thought about it the more he realised that it was not going to be easy for him to find a convenient opening and the less he trusted himself to do it diplomatically.

Wouldn't it be easier, he thought, for Simon, Arthur and Eleanor's son, to speak to Vera? Simon was living at home and saw her almost every day. But, although Simon also resented Vera's constant presence, feeling in his case that she stood between himself and his mother, he could not bring himself to speak to her either. In January 1961 Arthur shot himself.

In 1962 Michael McFall, Philippa's husband, formed a farming syndicate, with 11 partners from among those whose farms he was already managing. One of them was Sam's old colleague at Forsyth & Partners and at London & Coastal Oil Wharves, Sylvester Gates, who had a farm in Wiltshire. The farms totalled some two thousand acres and the project was favourably reported in *The Times*. The syndicate was run from Michael's own farm, Mallingdown, and Sam put Toll Farm into it, increasing his stake the following year by buying the Five Chimneys farm land, which lay the other side of Saxon Court. However, although the syndicate looked good on paper, it did not make profits and, in spite of the intention to pool resources, the farms were, in fact, too scattered and the accruing benefits were not enough to justify the high administration costs. Over the next few years, Sam kept an eye on it and the following entries appear in his diaries: 'examine the growth of debt in Mallingdown Farming Syndicate and try to reach some conclusion'; 'number of cattle increased but milk sales down' and 'badly paying enterprise'.

He was beginning to feel his age and the strain of keeping up Saxon Court was getting too much for him. Servants would not stay and the big kitchen with its Aga stove and large central wooden table, although warm, was not a comfortable place to sit or eat. When alone, they pushed trolleys to the dining room for their meals, but with the choice of Sam's library or one of the sitting rooms for the evening, there was no fixed place where he could relax and he was constantly jumping up to go in search of books or glasses which Kit had left in another room.

He suggested to Kit that they might move to Toll Farm House and offered to refurbish it for her. But she would not hear of going to live 'in such a small, ugly house so near the road'. She did agree, however, to consider the Elizabethan house of Five Chimneys Farm, which had a oasthouse and much the same south-facing view over the fields as Saxons. Encouraged, Sam got Winkfield Stutch-bury (Oliver's twin), who had an architectural practice in Lewes, to draw up plans for its modernisation.

In December 1962 Sam had his seventieth birthday, for which his five daughters and their husbands gave a party, attended by most of his grandchildren and a small number of his closest relations and friends. Determined to take life more easily, he wrote on the first page of his 1963 diary: 'Do not be shaken from your decision re. Saxon Court – get out before it kills you.'

XXV

Last Years In Cotton

Sam fought hard for the cotton industry all his life but he had no illusions that it would ever again be as important as it had been when he was a boy. He did not encourage his immediate family to invest in it and, unlike S. Noton Ltd, with which many of them were closely associated, he did not look upon it as providing for their future. However, in his chairman's statement to Cotton & Rayon Spinners in 1961 he was able to report that, thanks to the introduction of evening shifts, order books were full and that production was up some 30 per cent on the previous year. He was putting out feelers for more trade with Australia but already Australia was strengthening its ties with Japan as the UK turned to the European Common Market.

The limiting feature in production, he said, was now not orders, as was usually the case, but labour. Lancashire as a whole was working its machinery fewer hours than any other textile-producing country in the world 'due to the operatives' workload being determined on the basis of machinery long since out-dated and conditions long since past'.

Of the three mills that made up CARS, the Fernhurst and the Rugby were fully modernised but the third, the Delta, only partially. The Delta mill was spinning tubular yarn for use in surgical dressings but its re-equipment had not taken place because, Sam said, 'shift-working is not acceptable to the bulk of Lancashire operatives in spite of a half-hearted acceptance in principle of it by the Trade

Union leaders. Your Board', he continued, 'is now faced with the decision of whether or not to incur the very large expense of re-equipping it [the Delta Mill] throughout without some knowledge either that the new machinery will be worked to maximum capacity (and modern machinery necessitates shift working) or that the markets for our products will not continue to be eroded by unrestricted imports'.

As early as 1957 he had started a pension scheme for employees of Cotton & Rayon Spinners and when Sir Rupert De La Bere got in touch with him because his son-in-law was joining Noble Lowndes, who were looking to go into the pension scheme business, he was able to give the latter 'the opportunity of examining the [CARS] pension scheme'.

In 1962 he reported that the Cotton Board was compiling a list of mills agreeable to 'vertical links' and that he intended submitting CARS. He then referred again, as he had in 1956, to the horizontal stratification of the industry based on the bulk supply of staple goods for export markets, saying that the markets had gone but the outmoded organisation remained. 'The cotton industry', he said, 'has literally to be born again – machinery, labour, organisation – and it cannot successfully be born again if, during the process, it is exposed to unrestricted imports. It is commonly accepted that the successful development of a new industry requires protection. It is not so commonly understood that the necessary revolutionary changes to transfer the historically ancient Lancashire textile industry to meet modern conditions will be difficult to introduce without some protection.'

His report to Cotton & Rayon Spinners in 1964 was, however, a more optimistic one, in spite of there having been a big drop in yarn and cloth output from all Lancashire mills and more than 18,200 people having left the industry:

During the last decade, and particularly during the

175

last five years, the textile spinning trade has witnessed great changes. There have been fundamental improvements in machinery, outstanding inventions in new materials, well-nigh revolutionary changes in the application of labour and substantial alterations in the organisation of the industry itself. When we met at our last Annual General Meeting your Directors were alive to these changes and the vital part which they were bound to play in your future prospects but, having regard to the economic climate in which we were forced to operate, we were far from convinced that it was in the best interests of the shareholders of this Company to attempt to incorporate all these innovations in our own mills.

Since that time, two factors have influenced us to make up our minds. These are, on the one hand a more favourable economic climate and, on the other, the more understanding attitude by organised labour of the problems involved in our mutual task. So the die has been cast in favour of modernisation and, as we meet today, you find us in the midst of great and far-reaching changes in our set-up.

Among the changes he proposed, and which he said in his statement he felt would 'favourably affect our business prospects for many years to come', was the sale of the Fernhurst Mill, which he had been considering since 1962, and the concentration of all CARS production in one place.

He had been interested for some time in the Brunt Variable Speed Motor and was instrumental in setting up a company to develop it after the inventor, Charles Henry Brunt, who had received a premier award for it at the Brussels Exhibition, appealed to him for financial help. Brunt was made Managing Director of the company and Ronald Hardman (Sam's cousin's husband) a director. Sam thought that the motor only needed development to make it a money-spinner but its teething troubles were prolonged and in 1960 Hardman resigned, finding Brunt too difficult to work with.

Sam was confident that the motor could be used to drive spinning frames and, although Brunt Variable Speed Motors was losing money, he now got Cotton & Rayon Spinners and Tecalemit to invest in it. But by 1961 he had to report to the board of CARS that Charles Brunt had retired from the position of Managing Director, although he would remain as a consultant, and that CARS and Tecalemit would henceforth be equal partners in the company with Mr Scutt, the Managing Director of Tecalemit Ltd, as Chairman. Conversations with important textile engineers were under way, he reported, and there was also progress in other applications of the motor.

However, in 1962 Brunt Variable Speed Motors Ltd made a loss of over £35,000. In his report to the board of CARS Sam said: 'shareholders will share the disappointment of your Directors that the bright promise of the Brunt Motor is so late in coming to harvest. However, our confidence in the future of this motor is unabated.' But their confidence in Mr Brunt was not. 'Mr Brunt', Sam reported, 'has ceased to be employed by Brunt Variable Speed Motors Ltd in any capacity.' By 1964 confidence in the motor went too and the company was put into the hands of receivers.

XXVI

S. Noton Ltd

S. Noton Ltd had come a long way from its modest begin-
nings just after the First World War and Sam was proud
to have built it up, nursed it through the Depression of the
1930s and now, after the Second World War, to see it
prosper and expand. By 1958 there were seven S. Noton
subsidiaries, it had showrooms in Brook Street, Mayfair,
and a network of outlets across the world. In both 1960
and 1961 it increased its exports and in each of these years
declared a dividend of 16 per cent. In his report to the
board, Sam put stress particularly on the reliability of the
cases designed for air travel, many of which were now sold
with insurance and guarantees.

Production at Walthamstow was fully modernised,
thanks to the engineering skills of L.G. Polturak, who was
co-opted onto the board in 1961. He not only adapted
but also designed much of the machinery used and had
contacts with manufacturers in Milan. (For some years S.
Noton Ltd had a contract to produce luggage for Marks &
Spencer, who demanded very precise adherence to their
specifications.)

As an MP Sam had usually written his speeches out in
full, having them typed up by his secretary; but he also
made notes of the salient points, separated by dashes, and
had these on small pieces of card loosely joined at the
bottom so that, when he came to deliver the speech, he
could flip the cards over quickly. He prepared important
business speeches, such as his yearly chairman's reports, in
the same way.

Among his papers are notes for a report to the board of S. Noton Ltd: 'unlike the seers I speak for now not for eternity. For now (the next decade) the measure of achievement is the market. What works best, sells best. In the beginning it was sink or swim – we swam. Later it was compete or go under – we competed. Now it is excel or disappear – we excel.'

In 1962, although the second phase of building had to be postponed, the new extension to the factory was opened by the MP for Walthamstow and one-time mayor, and Parker Wakeling moved to Walthamstow. Production of both Crown and Victor luggage, for which new lines were announced for the following year, could now take place under the same roof and under L.G. Polturak's overall supervision.

Next Sam directed his thoughts towards sales. Since 1960 Noton's publicity had been in the hands of Newslines, owned and run by Geoffrey Lowis's daughter, Fiona Patterson, and advertisements appeared regularly, not only in trade papers but in all the leading glossy magazines. Max Wolsey, who was Joint Managing Director with Sam and a founder-member of the company, headed the Sales Service. Sam wrote to tell him of his long-term plans: 'We have a duty during our working lives to provide for succession', he wrote 'and the succession which I envisage for Notons, when you and I have departed from the scene is Michael White as sole Managing Director. Michael has been groomed for this position [this had included sending him on a management course to Ashridge College] and now that Parker Wakeling has moved to Walthamstow, with your help, he can be initiated into one further aspect of his work, namely the supervision of the management of the Noton's sales organisation.'

But in August 1962 Wolsey told Sam that he wanted to retire. However, although he resigned as Joint Managing Director, he was persuaded to stay on another year as Vice President. Parker Wakeling's site at Tottenham was sold and a resolution was passed to capitalise reserves by making a share issue of one for four.

In April 1963 Sam wrote to Michael White as follows: 'When you are the head of a business with varied activities, it is sometimes difficult to see the business as a whole; in consequence, things go wrong through a lack of balance.' He then gave him a list of the aspects of the business which should be kept constantly under review. These were: dynamic selling, efficient production, good buying, careful and conservative costing, quick distribution and considerate personnel management (low turnover of labour).

'Modern luggage', said Sam in his report for that year, 'is no longer merely a container, it is an attribute of fashion'. He also referred to added strength without added weight as 'a microcosm of scientific progress' and continued his report with: 'though the traditional markets of the British Commonwealth are gradually being barred to us (through imposition of quotas and restrictions by newly-emerging states) new markets in Europe and the Middle East open out encouraging prospects. Throughout the world there are customers who require the most sophisticated products that this technical age can produce.'

In 1964 he and Kit gave a party for Max and Mrs Wolsey on Max's retirement. Sam wanted to begin his speech by talking about the other founders of the company, Gold, Sharp, Rachow, Dix and his cousin Cyril, but Kit persuaded him that this would only be of nostalgic interest to him and Max and would make it too long for most of those present. The draft of this first speech is, however, among his papers, as well as the shorter version which he delivered.

Gold seldom spoke. He had, however, a very important function. He used to count the cases as they came off the production lines and endeavoured to reconcile this number with the number of cases that went out. How he did this nobody knew but an essential part of his equipment was an abacus, and the sight of Gold manipulating the coloured beads at tremendous speed was inspiring.

Sharp was a man of a different calibre. He had been brought up the hard way and was extremely careful of his own money and of the money belonging to the Company. He was in charge of purchases and our suppliers were under no misapprehension that Notons always bought in the cheapest market. He was honest as the day but even his best friends could not have called him sociable.

By far the most intellectual was Rachow. He was a gentle man; kindly, understanding and far-seeing. For years he suffered great pain with infinite fortitude. Unlike the other two, he inspired affection.

Dix was a man of very considerable charm and ability. He was an ambitious man. He had an inventive mind but he was the opposite of Sharp: he was not careful. He was generous with his own money and even more generous with the money of the Company. When the economic depression of the thirties overtook us, the clash of temperaments between Sharp and Dix was too great and Dix left us.

Cousin Cyril, wrote Sam, 'was not a business man. He cared a lot about golf and was very good at it. He found the atmosphere of our Directors Meetings in London most uncongenial and begged to be excused. Nevertheless, he looked after the Oldham branch with ability and care and always gave me the most loyal help. All these are dead and gone', he concluded, 'only Wolsey and I remain.'

Sam's statement to the board of S. Noton Ltd for 1964 must have given him considerable satisfaction. He was able to report that the year's trading had provided both a record turnover and a record profit, representing an increase of 16½ per cent in turnover and nearly 86 per cent in pre-tax profit.

Noton's business is the large-scale production of

luggage and similar articles. The industry has had to change from simple fabrication with wide tolerances to complicated machine production with narrow tolerances. The transference has been gradual and all the time it has been necessary to provide for highly competitive conditions. It will be appreciated, therefore, that the excellent result for the past year is not only the result of one year's working; it is the fruit of a long-term policy which should continue to be productive. In the manufacture of luggage our Development Department is second to none in Europe and a large number of the machines we use are built to our own design. It is pleasant to recall that the prophesy I made last year that Crown luggage for 1964 would be the best machine-made luggage that this country has produced, is now the record of a simple fact well recognised in the trade.

In November he set up a committee to implement Felix Polturak's recommendations for the company's computers. 'It was not a committee', he wrote to Michael White, 'to discuss whether computer technique would help Notons, but how it could be utilised. When I was a boy my father (who knew nothing of algebra) said he could solve all the problems with which he had to deal by arithmetic; and so he could, but there were a lot of problems he left unsolved. I am too old to speak with confidence about computer technique but I do know that it is here to stay. Our only choice is to include ourselves in.'

The year 1964 was very busy for Sam and very successful. However, it was not without its sadness: his great-nephew, Gyles Ryland, the only son of Gladys's daughter Joanna, died unexpectedly at the age of 26.

Sam and Kit already had 12 grandsons and 4 grand-daughters and saw them all regularly, often having one or more of the families down for the weekend. Sam, however, kept to his resolution to get out of Saxon Court. He put it on the market as early as July 1963, advertising it for sale in *Country Life* with a possible total of some 108 acres. He refurbished and let Toll Farm House and, with Winkie Stutchbury's alterations progressing nicely, he expected Five Chimneys to be ready for them to move into by the summer of 1965.

He did not, however, intend to retire, and by the end of the year was in contact with interested luggage-makers in South Africa with plans to capitalise on S. Noton's technical expertise in luggage-making by the sale of 'know-how' to them. In March 1965 he left for Johannesburg to enter into negotiations with the Hippo Manufacturing Co. Ltd. In the event, the Hippo company did not prove suitable for the manufacture of sophisticated suitcases. But by the end of his trip he had reached an agreement with a smaller organisation, Natal Leather Industries in Cape Town (which already had one of the necessary machines) that would give S. Noton Ltd a 50 per cent interest in their future output.

He then went to see Roy Welensky, the Prime Minister of Southern Rhodesia. A note in his handwriting says: 'having successfully finished my business with Welensky, I decided to push in a visit to Victoria Falls.' He had, however, already caught a chill 'due to a sudden drop in the temperature from 85 to 65 degrees' and on his way to the falls, a journey of some 500 miles of low flying in hot, steamy conditions, he 'felt very ill'. He put himself to bed in the hotel, had nothing to eat or drink (his throat was blocked with mucus so that he could not swallow) and on the following day returned to Salisbury. Anxious to get home as soon as possible and unable to get a direct flight, he returned to London via Lusaka and Lisbon. Dr Stuart Hensman admitted him to the St John's & St Elizabeth Hospital, where he was a consultant, but two weeks later, on 28 March 1965, after an unsuccessful operation, he died of a ruptured aneurysm.

'I shall never forget that loveable man', wrote one of his Jewish friends. 'He was a great source of inspiration to us and a great leader', wrote a business associate. Marta

Forsyth wrote of him as a 'wonderful person' and his hairdresser, Benedetto Viccari, wrote that he regarded Sam, who had been a client of his for so many years, as one of his very best friends. 'He brought to the House of Commons', wrote Lord Coleraine, 'great friendliness, an earthy commonsense and complete independence of mind'.

Three months previously Churchill's funeral had been watched by the whole country on television. When Sam's three-year-old granddaughter Sophia White was told that she was too young to go to the church for his funeral, she said: 'then can I watch it on television?' It was in fact a very simple affair, for the closest family only, at a country church near Saxons where Kit insisted that he be buried (although he had asked to be cremated) so that she in her turn could be buried beside him.

ACKNOWLEDGEMENTS

I wish to thank the following:

Miss Jean Ayton, archivist, for looking after my father's papers at Manchester Central Library.

Lord Coleraine for permission to use extracts from his father's unpublished memoirs.

Mr David Fletcher, Librarian of the Tank Museum, Bovington, for advice.

The Hon. Francis Noel-Baker for permission to quote from his father's letters to my mother.

Dr Henri Stellman for giving me access to early papers of the Anglo-Israel Association.

The Hon. Simon Stuart for discussions on the circumstances of his father's suicide and permission to publish my father's connection with it, as well as his own.

My sister Penelope Eckersley for permission to use two photographs of cotton mills from her husband Timothy's collection.

.

INDEX

191